LGBT Equality

ISSUES

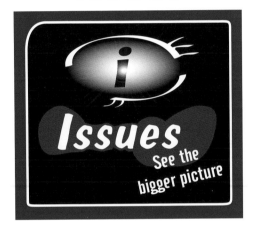

Volume 225

Series Editor

Lisa Firth

Independence

Educational Publishers

Cambridge

First published by Independence

The Studio, High Green

Great Shelford

Cambridge CB22 5EG

England

© Independence 2012

Photocopy licence

The material in this book is protected by copyright. However, the
purchaser is free to make multiple copies of particular articles for instructional
purposes for immediate use within the purchasing institution.
Making copies of the entire book is not permitted.

British Library Cataloguing in Publication Data

LGBT equality. -- (Issues ; v. 225)

1. Gays--Social conditions. 2. Sexual minorities.

I. Series II. Firth, Lisa.

306.7'6-dc23

ISBN-13: 978 1 86168 614 5

Printed in Great Britain

MWL Print Group Ltd

CONTENTS

Chapter 1 Sexual Orientation

Chapter 2 Trans Issues

Chapter 3 LGBT People and the Law

OTHER TITLES IN THE ISSUES SERIES

For more on these titles, visit: www.independence.co.uk

The Internet Revolution ISBN 978 1 86168 451 6
An Ageing Population ISBN 978 1 86168 452 3
Poverty and Exclusion ISBN 978 1 86168 453 0
Waste Issues ISBN 978 1 86168 454 7
Staying Fit ISBN 978 1 86168 455 4
The AIDS Crisis ISBN 978 1 86168 468 4
Bullying Issues ISBN 978 1 86168 469 1
Marriage and Cohabitation ISBN 978 1 86168 470 7
Privacy and Surveillance ISBN 978 1 86168 472 1
The Animal Rights Debate ISBN 978 1 86168 473 8
Body Image and Self-Esteem ISBN 978 1 86168 484 4
Abortion – Rights and Ethics ISBN 978 1 86168 485 1
Racial and Ethnic Discrimination ISBN 978 1 86168 486 8
Sexual Health ISBN 978 1 86168 487 5
Selling Sex ISBN 978 1 86168 488 2
Citizenship and Participation ISBN 978 1 86168 489 9
Health Issues for Young People ISBN 978 1 86168 500 1
Reproductive Ethics ISBN 978 1 86168 502 5
Tackling Child Abuse ISBN 978 1 86168 503 2
Money and Finances ISBN 978 1 86168 504 9
The Housing Issue ISBN 978 1 86168 505 6
Teenage Conceptions ISBN 978 1 86168 523 0
Work and Employment ISBN 978 1 86168 524 7
Understanding Eating Disorders ISBN 978 1 86168 525 4
Student Matters ISBN 978 1 86168 526 1
Cannabis Use ISBN 978 1 86168 527 8
Health and the State ISBN 978 1 86168 528 5
Tobacco and Health ISBN 978 1 86168 539 1
The Homeless Population ISBN 978 1 86168 540 7
Coping with Depression ISBN 978 1 86168 541 4
The Changing Family ISBN 978 1 86168 542 1
Bereavement and Grief ISBN 978 1 86168 543 8
Endangered Species ISBN 978 1 86168 544 5
Responsible Drinking ISBN 978 1 86168 555 1
Alternative Medicine ISBN 978 1 86168 560 5
Censorship Issues ISBN 978 1 86168 558 2
Living with Disability ISBN 978 1 86168 557 5
Sport and Society ISBN 978 1 86168 559 9
Self-Harming and Suicide ISBN 978 1 86168 556 8
Sustainable Transport ISBN 978 1 86168 572 8
Mental Wellbeing ISBN 978 1 86168 573 5
Child Exploitation ISBN 978 1 86168 574 2
The Gambling Problem ISBN 978 1 86168 575 9
The Energy Crisis ISBN 978 1 86168 576 6
Nutrition and Diet ISBN 978 1 86168 577 3
Coping with Stress ISBN 978 1 86168 582 7
Consumerism and Ethics ISBN 978 1 86168 583 4

Genetic Modification ISBN 978 1 86168 584 1
Education and Society ISBN 978 1 86168 585 8
The Media ISBN 978 1 86168 586 5
Biotechnology and Cloning ISBN 978 1 86168 587 2
International Terrorism ISBN 978 1 86168 592 6
The Armed Forces ISBN 978 1 86168 593 3
Vegetarian Diets ISBN 978 1 86168 594 0
Religion in Society ISBN 978 1 86168 595 7
Tackling Climate Change ISBN 978 1 86168 596 4
Euthanasia and Assisted Suicide ISBN 978 1 86168 597 1
A Sustainable Future ISBN 978 1 86168 603 9
Class and Social Mobility ISBN 978 1 86168 604 6
Population Growth and Migration ISBN 978 1 86168 605 3
Equality and Gender Roles ISBN 978 1 86168 606 0
Tourism and Travel ISBN 978 1 86168 607 7
Crime, Punishment and Justice ISBN 978 1 86168 608 4
Domestic and Relationship Abuse ISBN 978 1 86168 613 8
LGBT Equality ISBN 978 1 86168 614 5
Globalisation and Trade ISBN 978 1 86168 615 2
Ethics in Business ISBN 978 1 86168 616 9
Illegal Drug Use ISBN 978 1 86168 617 6
Protecting Human Rights ISBN 978 1 86168 618 3

A note on critical evaluation

Because the information reprinted here is from a number of different sources, readers should bear in mind the origin of the text and whether the source is likely to have a particular bias when presenting information (just as they would if undertaking their own research). It is hoped that, as you read about the many aspects of the issues explored in this book, you will critically evaluate the information presented. It is important that you decide whether you are being presented with facts or opinions. Does the writer give a biased or an unbiased report? If an opinion is being expressed, do you agree with the writer?

LGBT Equality offers a useful starting point for those who need convenient access to information about the many issues involved. However, it is only a starting point. Following each article is a URL to the relevant organisation's website, which you may wish to visit for further information.

Chapter 1

SEXUAL ORIENTATION

Am I gay? Are you born gay? Can you stop being gay?

Information from AVERT.

Am I gay?

Many people feel attracted to people of the same sex, and wonder whether this means that they are gay. For some people these feelings can be very intense and alienating. Some people who ask themselves the question 'am I gay?' are indeed gay, and go on to have gay sexual relationships. But other people find that these feelings change over time.

Some people are bisexual, meaning they are attracted to both men and women, and have relationships with both. Some people are not attracted to anyone and wonder if this is a sign that they are gay. Often it is only time that will resolve these uncertainties.

When do people know that they are gay?

There is no simple answer to this question, as it varies from person to person. Deciding you are gay often happens gradually, it may not be something you can initially put a name to, and it can feel very confusing.

During research carried out with young gay men in the UK, the men interviewed described a set of feelings which they gradually realised made them 'different' in some way, feelings they thought maybe every teenage boy has.

'I thought, well, this is just the phase bit. Sooner or later I'm going to start finding women attractive. I never did. As I became more attracted to men, and I still wasn't getting attracted to women, I thought, s**t, you're gay. And it was really quite a shock when it hit me.' *Luke*

With time, someone who is gay will realise that not only are they sexually attracted to members of the same sex, but that this attraction is not transitional. This realisation could come at any time during their lives. Many people become aware of gay feelings during their teenage years, as this is when they begin to learn more about their sexuality and identity. However, the difficulties associated with accepting these feelings and coming out mean that many gay people don't identify themselves as gay until much later on in life.

'After college I spent nearly 15 years trying to deny to myself who I was ... a gay man. Finally, at age 38, I began to accept the fact that I was gay.'

Is being gay a phase young people go through?

For some people yes, and for others, no.

Some people do not have their first homosexual feelings or experience until they are well into adulthood. In a survey on sexual feelings carried out in Britain, nearly the same number of women reported that their first homosexual experience had happened in their twenties as did in their thirties, forties or fifties.

There is evidence that for some people homosexual experiences are part of a transitional or experimental phase in their youth. This is hardly surprising given that adolescence is a period of change in which many people find who they are and what they want for themselves in adult life. This kind of behaviour is perfectly normal.

Are you born gay? What causes people to be gay?

There is no simple answer to the question, 'Are some people born lesbian or gay?' There are some theories that stress biological differences between heterosexual and homosexual adults, suggesting that people are born with their sexuality already determined.

The American researcher Dean Hamer published research that seemed to prove that homosexual orientation could be genetically transmitted to men on the x chromosome, which they get from their mothers. However, when this study was duplicated it did not produce the same results. A follow-up study which Hamer collaborated on also failed to reinforce his earlier results.

Subsequent research published by George Rice and George Ebers of the University of Western Ontario has

AVERT

cast doubt on Hamer's theory. Rice and Ebers' research also tested the same region of the x chromosome in a larger sample of gay men, but failed to find the same 'marker' that Hamer's research had found. Claims that the part of the brain known as the hypothalamus is influential in determining sexual orientation have yet to be substantiated. It is generally thought that biological explanations of sexuality are insufficient to explain the diversity of human sexuality.

'How can science tell you what I am? I mean I've had boyfriends, and was happy with them, had girlfriends and may have boyfriends again for all I know. If it's a gay gene what's going on? Is it just turning itself on and off in my head? It doesn't feel like biology, it feels like love.' *Jo*

In a survey on sexual feelings carried out in Britain, nearly the same number of women reported that their first homosexual experience had happened in their twenties as did in their thirties, forties or fifties

---

Psycho-social explanations offer a variety of factors that could contribute to the development of a person's homosexuality. For example, a female-dominated upbringing in a gay man's past, with an absence of a male role model. Others stress adherence or deviance from conformity to gender roles, and individual psychological makeup. While none of these factors alone completely answers the question 'what causes homosexuality?', they rule out some things. For example, lesbian and gay young people are not 'failed' heterosexuals. Also, homosexual partners are generally of the same age, proving wrong the assumptions that young people are 'turned gay' by older people.

What is clear is that people's behaviour is influenced by their family environment, their experiences and their sense of themselves. Beliefs about sex are initially shaped by family values. Later on these beliefs may be shaped by pleasant and unpleasant experiences of sex and also shape their choice of activities and partners. Throughout their life a person's sense of who and what they are has a strong impact on their sexual development and experience.

Can you stop being gay?

There is now growing general support for the belief that sexuality is pre-determined, though may change over time. However, many people are interested in whether sexuality can be altered solely by a person's desire to change. Organisations that help homosexuals attempt to change their sexuality can be generally divided between those that use psychological 'reparative' methods and those that use religious 'healing' methods.

Some people believe homosexuality is an illness and believe it can and should be cured. Many of these 'cures' revolve around psychological therapies (often called reparative therapy) which endeavour to re-orient a homosexual sexuality to heterosexual. Although there is little scientific data to evaluate, what is available seems to indicate that reparative therapy is ineffective. The American Psychological Association (APA), the world's largest association of psychologists, has stated that:

'Homosexuality is not a mental disorder and the APA opposes all portrayals of lesbian, gay and bisexual people as mentally ill and in need of treatment due to their sexual orientation.'

Some strongly religious groups believe that homosexuality is sinful and is in direct breach of the Bible and other religious texts. As with reparative therapy, there has been little to no scientific evaluation of the healing and prayer techniques used. What evidence is available suggests that the success of these techniques is restricted to three areas:

⇨ Convincing bisexuals to limit their sexual activities to members of the opposite sex.

⇨ Convincing homosexuals to become celibate.

⇨ Convincing gay men and lesbians to attempt to maintain heterosexual relationships, whilst retaining their homosexual orientation.

Tellingly, two founders of a ministry established to 'heal' homosexuals later described their programme as 'ineffective ... not one person was healed'.

The subject of 'curing' homosexuality became a politically charged debate in America, with Christian political organisations promoting the theory that homosexuality can be changed through force of will alone. They claim that 'thousands are leaving their homosexual identity for sexual celibacy, and even marriage'.

Alternatively, gay and lesbian rights organisations would argue that these views misunderstand what it means to be gay, and amount to discrimination against gay and lesbian people. Furthermore, the APA has carried out a systematic review, which not only concludes that psychological interventions are not effective at changing sexual orientation, but they can also cause significant harm.

⇨ The above information is reprinted with kind permission from AVERT. Please visit www.avert.org for more, or to view references for this piece.

AVERT

Parents' stories

The families of gay and lesbian young people share their experiences of learning about their relative's orientation.

Janet J's Story

The day started out normally enough. Glyn, 19, was home from university for the weekend. He was due to leave on the Sunday afternoon, so we went out for an early pub lunch. My husband and I both had our mouths full of roast beef when, in a quiet voice, Glyn broke the silence with 'I've got something to tell you – I'm gay'. Now, some parents say they already had their suspicions, but not us, not an inkling. The thoughts rushed through my head: what had we done to cause this, had I mothered him too much? Was this a passing phase? Glyn assured us that he'd known since his early teens that he was gay, and that he was sure it was just the way he was born. After all, his older brother was brought up in the same way and he was straight. Then the worries set in: surely he'd be dead with AIDS before the year was out; if not that, then he'd get beaten up every time he went out. He'd always be sad and lonely, and would be discriminated against in every aspect of life.

Glyn had obviously thought about our likely reactions and tried to allay our fears, but as soon as we'd left him at the station, the tears flowed. It felt a bit like bereavement, a grieving for the life I'd had planned for him: the happy and successful life, the daughter-in-law, the grandchildren. When we got home, my husband (much calmer than me!) suggested we sit down and write a list of 'what could be worse'. That soon put things into perspective. We thought of other young people we knew who were suffering from mental or life-threatening illnesses, or who were into a life of alcohol, drug abuse or crime – and just being gay suddenly didn't look so bad.

Like many women, I needed to talk – a lot! I was fortunate to have friends I could turn to but, best of all, I found FFLAG – Families and Friends of Lesbians and Gay Men. It was wonderful to talk to someone who knew just how I felt. Once I'd come to terms with Glyn's sexuality, I decided to help establish the first helpline and support group in Wales, and it's been wonderful to have been able to help so many other mums and dads over the years to realise that their child's sexuality is only a small part of their life, and that they are still the same dearly-loved child they always were. We say that being gay is just like being left-handed – a bit unusual, a bit inconvenient at times, but in general not a major problem. And Glyn – he's been with his lovely partner for nine years now, they've bought a house together, he has a successful career and lots of friends. It's all good now!

A sister's story

My 'little sister' came out over 14 years ago. She was married, although separated from her husband, and had a young son. It simply never occurred to me that she was anything other than heterosexual. The only thing that upset me on hearing her news, was that I felt that somehow I should have known. I felt guilty that I had not been more supportive and I really worried that she had been very unhappy over the years.

Our parent's reaction was initially hostile and very negative. I was living hundreds of miles away at the time, and know that my sister had a very difficult time of it. Our father would put the phone down if my sister's partner happened to answer it. Our mother often became quite hysterical and tearful. Gradually things changed and they adjusted to the fact that one of their daughters happened to be a lesbian. And over the years they came to love my sister's partner as a true member of the family too.

What saddens me is that various pressures mean that neither my sister nor her partner is 'out' at work. My sister works for a multi-national company and says that if her work colleagues found out that she was gay she would lose respect and her authority. For me, my little sister's sexuality is not an issue. It's not something I think about. However, I know that life is still not as easy as it should be for my sister and her partner. The other day we were discussing the fact that they need a new bed. Bed manufacturers recommend that you and your partner test the suitability of the mattress by lying on it in the shop. I said that I thought this was a good idea – and she looked askance at me. 'What do you think they would say in the shop if Liz and I lay down on the bed together?' It simply hadn't occurred to me that anyone would take issue or that my sister and her partner would be uncomfortable doing that. I have a lot to learn!

Bruce's story

For most of my adult life I have been involved in charismatic Christian churches and was a pastor for many years. We brought our five children up to follow the Scriptures and it never occurred to us that one might be gay. One day, however, I felt a strong inner conviction that one of my sons was gay. This caused great inner turmoil and I didn't say anything about it to anyone for a long time but it led me to begin to quietly research what homosexuality is and what the Bible actually teaches about it.

FFLAG

My understanding at the time had been that homosexuality was a perversion brought about by wrong family relationships like a remote, uncaring father figure and an oppressive, dominant mother figure. Although this didn't really describe our family, I knew there had been too many times when I had been off 'looking after the flock' rather than with my family. So I was going through a personal hell, battling a sense of guilt as well as shame. Next I went through a period of mourning. I would like to say this was an unselfish mourning for our son and the difficulties he was going through but the truth is it was mostly selfish. How was I going to tell my wife, family and friends? What would the church think and what would become of my ministry?

> **'Gradually things changed and [my parents] adjusted to the fact that one of their daughters happened to be a lesbian. And over the years they came to love my sister's partner as a true member of the family too'**

It seemed to me that there were three fundamental barriers to understanding the truth.

1   The thought that surely the Church can't all be wrong on this issue.

2   The conviction that it is unnatural to have same-sex attraction.

3   Anyway, the Bible clearly condemns it.

Number 1 barrier was easy. The 'Church' has rarely all agreed on anything. In fact, the 'Church' has invariably got it badly wrong – from the days of the Apostles when they thought slavery was okay, even to today when most denominations still don't treat women as equals to men.

Number 2 barrier was easily enough to hurdle intellectually but more difficult emotionally. It didn't take much study to discover that homosexuality occurs naturally throughout the animal kingdom. For some people, attraction to the opposite sex is natural for them. The difficult part was that, for me, homosexual sex seemed disturbingly unpleasant. But then I remembered when my older sister had told me about the 'birds and the bees' when I was quite young and how revolted I had felt about what she had described at the time.

Number 3 barrier came as a bombshell when I understood that so many of us charismatics had been fundamentally interpreting the Scriptures wrongly, and the way we understood it to teach against homosexuality was just symptomatic.

The Bible is written to point us towards faith in Jesus. There are a lot of things taught in the Bible that we know would be wrong for us to adopt today, such as polytheism, owning slaves, the death penalty for breaking religious laws, oppressing women, ethnic cleansing and genocide as well as persecution of gays. We need to interpret the Old and the New Testaments in the light of God's law of love. Actually, the Biblical writers had no concept of a loving, faithful, stable gay relationship between two men or two women and so they never addressed the matter.

When my son did eventually come to me to tell me he was gay, by God's grace I had come through most of my negative emotions and was able to hug him and tell him that I loved him and that I was fully supportive of him. It wasn't plain sailing after that though. I told his Mum first and she cried for a long time. His brothers and sisters had serious problems with it and to some degree still do, although we all try to be loving towards each other.

I resigned from pastoring the AOG church so that I could speak freely about this and other issues. My website www.love-amazing.com is my way of standing up for the truth as I understand it. My wife and I joined FFLAG and it is a real joy to be able help, even in a small way, parents who are going through the same traumas that we went through. Being a part of FFLAG has been enormously encouraging to us because we have met so many caring people who have wisdom and compassion that has been borne out of pain.

⇨ The above information is reprinted with kind permission from Families and Friends of Lesbians and Gay Men (FFLAG). Visit www.fflag.org.uk for more information.

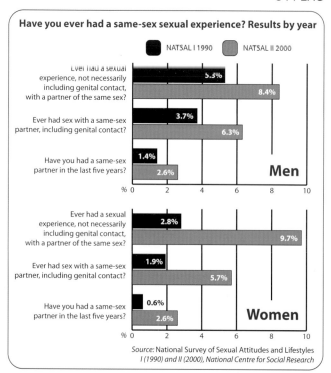

Have you ever had a same-sex sexual experience? Results by year

NATSAL I 1990   NATSAL II 2000

Men

	NATSAL I 1990	NATSAL II 2000
Ever had a sexual experience, not necessarily including genital contact, with a partner of the same sex?	5.3%	8.4%
Ever had sex with a same-sex partner, including genital contact?	3.7%	6.3%
Have you had a same-sex partner in the last five years?	1.4%	2.6%

Women

	NATSAL I 1990	NATSAL II 2000
Ever had a sexual experience, not necessarily including genital contact, with a partner of the same sex?	2.8%	9.7%
Ever had sex with a same-sex partner, including genital contact?	1.9%	5.7%
Have you had a same-sex partner in the last five years?	0.6%	2.6%

Source: National Survey of Sexual Attitudes and Lifestyles I (1990) and II (2000), National Centre for Social Research

FFLAG

Being LGB or T at school

Frequently asked questions on schooling for lesbian, gay, bisexual and transgender children and young people.

Which children are lesbian, gay, bisexual or transgender (LGBT)?

The short answer is that you cannot tell from looking at someone whether or not they identify as lesbian, gay, bisexual or transgender (LGBT). LGBT people come from all walks of life, are black, brown, white and all shades in between, achieve across all levels of educational attainment, may or may not be disabled; they make up part of the broad spectrum of humanity. Some children may look or dress differently to their peers but this, in itself, does not mean that they identify as LGBT, or that they will when they are older. Some children may not have thought about their sexual or gender identities yet, while others may be unsure. For some, their sexual or gender identity may change over time. Children who have LGBT parents/carers are no more, and no less, likely than children with heterosexual or gender-normative (see footnote on p8) parents/carers to be LGBT themselves. It is also important to recognise that there is a great deal of diversity in terms of how individuals self-identify their sexual and gender identities within the LGBT communities and that the terms lesbian, gay, bisexual and transgender are not adopted by everyone. For example, some people may prefer to call themselves queer, neutrois or pansexual.

What is meant by 'transgender'?

The term 'transgender', which is often abbreviated to 'trans', is an 'umbrella' term for people whose gender identity and/or gender expression differs from their birth sex. Some trans people feel themselves to be unambiguously male or female, and may or may not be recognised by others as such. Some people may adopt the term transsexual. Others feel that their gender identities are not adequately encompassed by either of the gender options available within a binary gender system (for example, man or woman, male or female) and may use a variety of terms to describe themselves, including un-gendered, genderqueer, gender bent, queer or simply human. People who cross-dress or identify as transvestite might also describe themselves, or be described by others, as being transgender. Some intersex people may go on to transition to the gender with which they identify in later life if they feel that they were assigned to the wrong gender as a baby. Transitioning is the term used to describe someone changing from one gender to another, or moving to their 'acquired' gender. This may be done with or without medical interventions, such as hormones or surgery. Some trans people do not like this concept, arguing that their gender identity has never changed and that they have not 'acquired' a new one. The terms 'gender reassignment' and 'acquired gender', however, are exclusively used within legislation (such as the Gender Recognition Act) and dominate the medical community's understanding of trans identities.

Why is transgender grouped alongside lesbian, gay and bisexual in the acronym LGBT?

While it is important to understand that gender and sexual identity are different characteristics of human identity and experience, they are often intertwined within political campaigning, activism, popular consciousness and school policy. Deviation from heterosexuality and deviation from gender normativity are often greeted with equally hostile responses, with both being 'lumped' together as suitably Other. People may assume a person is LGB or T because they look or behave differently to the way in which their culture feels it is acceptable for a person of that birth sex to behave. People from within the LGB and T communities adopt a range of views over whether or not each of these groupings should go together. Some feel that there is no common ground and would prefer that the T is not included (or even that lesbians, gay men and bisexuals all self-organise separately) while others feel that there is strength in numbers and recognise that LGBT people often experience discrimination and bullying because they may be seen to challenge conventional ideas of gender. It is also worth remembering that some trans people may also identify as lesbian, gay or bisexual and that many trans people experience homophobia from people who incorrectly associate their gender identity with homosexuality.

We don't have any LGBT people in our school so why do we need to know about them?

In 2004 it was estimated that there were 124,672 same-gender-attracted pupils in British secondary schools (Warwick et al., 2004). This is approximately 100 pupils in a school of 2,000. Children of primary school age may identify as lesbian, gay or bisexual or may go on to as they develop. Gender variance may be detected in children as young as two, and among pre-pubertal pupils there are likely to be 60 in 1,000 who will experience non-heterosexuality that may be difficult to distinguish from 'atypical' gender identity, while in any school of 1,000 pupils there are likely to be six who will experience

CENTRE FOR STUDIES ON INCLUSIVE EDUCATION

transgenderism throughout their lives. A high proportion of people who undergo gender reassignment as adults say that they knew that they were trans while in primary school, even if they lacked the language to express this (Reed et al., 2008).

Figures vary over how many adults identify as lesbian, gay or bisexual but an estimate that is often used is the figure of one in ten. There may be more who engage in same-gender sexual activities but identify as heterosexual. The number of transgender people within the UK is relatively small but the figures are growing as more people feel able to be open about who they are. One study (Reed et al., 2009) estimates there to be 500,000 transgender adults. Some of these may also identify as lesbian, gay or bisexual.

LGBT people – both children and adults – may be less visible within a school than their heterosexual and gender normative peers. This may be because it feels unsafe for them to be open about who they are, but does not mean that they do not exist. In addition to members of a school community who identify as LGBT themselves, there will also be those who have LGBT members in their immediate or extended family and/or friends.

Part of the rationale of schooling is to prepare children and young people for life in the wider world. LGBT people make up a significant part of our society and schools are failing their pupils if they do not educate them about the important role LGBT people have always played, and will continue to play, in the shaping of our society. CSIE believes that everyone is of equal value, earned by virtue of being human. We believe that diversity is part of what makes the world beautiful; it should be celebrated and utilised as a rich learning resource. Everyone should be valued and made to feel welcome.

As for resources and training, of course they help. Accessing resources and training often requires funds, time and will (and we all know what happens 'when there is a will'.) Principles underpinning 'special education', however, are not all that different from principles underpinning 'education'. Many mainstream school staff have been pleasantly surprised to find that creative ways to respond to the diversity of learners often emerge from their own resourceful thinking, sometimes in consultation with external agencies, always in consultation with young people and their families. This is not to say that inclusion is easy. But it is possible.

What is the legal position with regard to LGBT people in schools?

The Equality Act (2010) tackles disadvantage and discrimination based on sex, gender reassignment and sexual orientation amongst other protected characteristics. The basic framework offers protection against direct and indirect discrimination, harassment and victimisation in services and public functions. As such, it imposes a duty on all public bodies (including schools and academies) to be proactive in promoting equality of opportunity for all. The Act repeals the Sex Discrimination Act (1975) and the Gender Equality Duty (GED). The Act offers greater protection on the grounds of gender reassignment than existing equality law as it protects:

⇨ trans people who are not under medical supervision (this may have particular relevance for young trans people who are often told that they are too young to alter their bodies should they wish to do so);

⇨ people who experience discrimination because they are perceived to be trans;

⇨ people who experience discrimination by association of gender reassignment (for example, it would protect a child who experiences discrimination because one of their parents is transitioning).

The Act similarly supersedes much previous legislation that protects LGBT staff or adults, updating the Employment Equality (Sexual Orientation) Regulations (2003) that requires schools to ensure that LGB staff are not subject to direct or indirect discrimination.

The Gender Recognition Act (2004) still stands and provides some trans people with legal recognition for their 'acquired' gender. Legal recognition follows from the issue of a full Gender Recognition Certificate by a Gender Recognition Panel. This may apply to some members of staff or to parents/carers of children in a school.

Have you ever had a same-sex sexual experience? Results by age

■ 16-17 years ■ 18-19 years □ 20-24 years ■ Average, 16-24 years

Men

Ever had a sexual experience with a same-sex partner?
- 1.2%
- 5.6%
- 6.3%
- 4.3%

Ever had sexual intercourse/genital contact with a same-sex partner?
- 1.2%
- 2.3%
- 4.2%
- 2.6%

% 0 1 2 3 4 5 6 7

Women

Ever had a sexual experience with a same-sex partner?
- 5.1%
- 9.7%
- 12.6%
- 9.1%

Ever had sexual intercourse/genital contact with a same-sex partner?
- 2.5%
- 4.6%
- 6.5%
- 4.5%

% 0 3 6 9 12 15

Source: National Survey of Sexual Attitudes and Lifestyles II (2000), National Centre for Social Research

CENTRE FOR STUDIES ON INCLUSIVE EDUCATION

The Human Rights Act (1998) is still in force and requires schools to respect and value all of their pupils. Specific provisions include the right to a private and family life (which includes LGBT families), freedom from discrimination, and the right to education. The Equal Opportunity Commission highlighted sexist and sexual bullying in 2007 as an issue in implementing the GED. Under the GED public authorities had to demonstrate that they were promoting equality for girls/women and boys/men (including LGBT girls/women and boys/men) and that they were working to eliminate sexual discrimination and harassment. The GED specifically noted that homophobia in a school setting restricts the implementation of this Duty. Work carried out by schools under the GED will now continue under the Equality Act.

In addition to the Equality Act there are a number of other pieces of legislation that relate specifically to schools concerning pupil behaviour and bullying. Section 61 of the School Standard and Framework Act (1998) imposes a duty on governing bodies to ensure that policies intended to promote good behaviour and pupil discipline are enacted at a school. They must also regularly review a written statement of general principles used by the headteacher to encourage good behaviour and respect for others, particularly in relation to preventing all forms of bullying.

The Education and Inspection Act 2006 draws on the Education Act (2002) and the Schools Inspection Act (1996). The need to safeguard and promote the rights and welfare of pupils is clearly laid out in section 117(2). Section 89(5) allows all teachers to impose disciplinary penalties for inappropriate behaviour and gives head teachers the power to control the behaviour of pupils outside of school 'To such extent as is reasonable.'

Ofsted's duties for inspecting schools are outlined in *The evaluation schedule for schools* (Ofsted, 2010). Where a school is failing to enforce the range of legislation outlined above, inspectors have the power to raise this in their reports. Schools are then legally obliged to act or face penalties, the most extreme of which is closure. More proactively, schools may use sexualities and gender equality work as part of the process for securing a nationally recognised Inclusion Quality Mark, much valued by Ofsted.

We think that it is inappropriate to talk to very young children about sex so how can we possibly deal with LGBT issues in the classroom?

The age at which schools speak to children about sex is a matter for individual bodies to discuss in consultation with parent and governor groups. However, children talk about sex from an early age within the playground and references to sex exist in abundance within popular culture. Schools therefore often feel that it is advisable to educate their pupils so that misinformation can be dispelled. This can and should be done in an age-appropriate manner. As such, it is unlikely that any school will be teaching very young children about the mechanics of having sex: rather, it is more likely that schools wish to encourage pupils to adopt values about the importance of respect and the promotion of healthy relationships. Lesbian, gay and bisexual relationships, and LGBT identities more broadly, can and should be raised alongside the teaching of heterosexual relationships and gendered identities. This can be done in an entirely habitual manner and there are a number of resources available to help schools initiate discussions. It is important to remember that the Civil Partnership Act (2005) places a duty on schools to recognise the existence of families based on same-sex partnerships, and to discuss these families as confidently and regularly as they do others. It is important that children from LGBT families feel that their families are recognised, accepted and respected. It is entirely appropriate that discussions amongst very young children revolve around the diversity of families that exist within our society. This is one very simple way in which schools can speak about LGBT identities without talking about sex.

How should schools respond to the multiple uses of the word 'gay'?

Any use of the term 'gay' to mean that something is nonsense, broken or otherwise sub-standard should not be tolerated amongst pupils or staff. CSIE believes that the use of the term in this way is homophobic and is therefore inappropriate within a school setting. Pupils and staff should be encouraged to find alternative expressions that do not castigate a particular sexual identity. A lot of people would not dream of uttering a religious or racial slur. Being lesbian, gay or bisexual is often viewed negatively. Failing to challenge the use of this phrase in this manner gives further credence to this view. Schools should think about how to respond to such comments and ensure that all members of staff are equally committed to eradicating its usage in such a context. Simultaneously, however, schools need to create safe environments where it is alright for people to talk openly about gay identities without fear of being labelled homophobic. Gay identities are both entirely usual and a source of pride. One way in which this may be facilitated is for schools to engage with LGBT History Month.

What is transphobia?

Transphobia is a term used to describe discrimination that can be experienced by trans people, people who are thought to be trans, or people who may have trans family and friends as a result of the way in which a person expresses their gender identity. Schools should ensure that anti-bullying policies address both homophobia and transphobia, while also making sure that staff and

children are aware of the differences and overlaps between the two and feel confident in responding to each. Homophobic and transphobic incidents are both regarded as hate crimes within the legal system.

What should we do as school staff if a pupil comes out to us as being LGBT?

Young people come out to staff for a variety of reasons. These may include, but are by no means limited to, a need for pastoral support, a desire for information or redress for how they are being treated. Young people have told us that they find it helpful when staff thank them for sharing this information with them. For some young people this may be the first time that they have ever verbalised their LGBT identity and the process may be nerve-wracking. Young people have also said that they find it helpful when staff listen to them and ask them why they have shared this information. For example, a young person may tell a member of staff that they are trans because they do not know who to turn to for information about transitioning, while another may disclose that they are bisexual because they do

not feel their specific needs for information around safer sex are being met within the Sex and Relationship Education programme. Who, if anyone, the member of staff shares such a disclosure with depends upon the specific context, while individual schools have established child protection policies. These should be adhered to at all times.

Why do so many LGBT pupils get bullied?

While this group of children and young people (or those perceived to be, or with family or friends who are LGBT) face a very real and disproportionate level of violence and hatred within primary and secondary schools (see for example Guasp, 2010; Hunt and Jensen, 2007; Whittle et al., 2007), it is by no means inevitable that they will be bullied. However, where they are bullied this is often due to the wider culture of the school, either turning a blind eye, or failing to challenge heterosexist and gender normative ways of thinking. It is the duty of all members of staff to ensure that every child is valued and respected within school. Inclusive schools enable young people to be happy irrespective of who they are attracted to or what they look like. Where schools foster safe, welcoming and respectful atmospheres, and where diversity is genuinely valued, homophobia and transphobia are significantly reduced, if not eliminated entirely.

> You are definitely challenging our ideas of normality.

> Maybe you should try updating your ideas?

Footnote

When a person is born they are assigned a gender by a doctor, midwife and/or parent/carer. This assignation is based on the appearance of the baby's genitals (for example, vulva and clitoris = girl). Some people are born with ambiguous genitalia or have sex chromosomal variations that may be detected during puberty or even later in life, but they too are assigned a gender at birth. It is generally assumed that the gender assigned to a baby will be the gender that that person will grow up to be. This is called **gender normativity**. People who challenge gender normativity may feel that the gender assigned to them at birth is wrong or that it fails to adequately express how they conceive of their gender identity – for example, people who identify as intersex, transsexual, transgender, gender questioning or genderqueer may all be said to challenge ideas of gender normativity.

Updated 4 February 2011

⇨ The above information is an extract from information produced by the Centre for Studies on Inclusive Education and is reprinted with their kind permission. Please visit www.csie.org.uk for more information.

© CSIE

CENTRE FOR STUDIES ON INCLUSIVE EDUCATION

Social exclusion and sexual orientation

Information from Stonewall.

Overview

There is limited evidence relating to sexual orientation and economic circumstances.

The general perception, often perpetuated by the media, that the majority of the 'gay community' is mainly white, male and middle-class, with high levels of disposable income, does not accurately reflect the diverse backgrounds of gay people in Britain.

Lesbian, gay and bisexual people are of course just as likely to be from low-income backgrounds as any other demographic. Gay people from more affluent demographics are simply more visible than those from other backgrounds.

It is also well documented that discrimination can lead to social exclusion. Therefore gay people are in fact likely to experience greater economic deprivation and social exclusion in some circumstances precisely because of their sexual orientation.

The business case for diversity

Lesbians, gay men and bisexuals are an important part of the talent pool ...

⇨ Lesbians, gay men and bisexuals comprise around 6% of the population, or 3.5 million people, according to government estimates.

⇨ 36% of gay employees will change careers if discrimination is continued.

⇨ A third of gay staff conceal their sexual orientation from their employers and co-workers, yet 'out' employees in safe environments earn 50% more than their closeted peers.

⇨ At least 55% of gay employees facing discrimination report a direct negative work impact.

⇨ Approximately 20% of gay employees facing discrimination at work will consider suicide.

... and an important market

⇨ The 'pink pound' is estimated to be worth £70 billion.

⇨ 74% of gay and 42% of straight consumers are less likely to buy products from companies that hold negative views of lesbians and gay men.

© BITC Diversity: www.bitcdiversity.org.uk

What we know

No-one knows how many gay people there are in Britain. Due to the legacy of criminalisation and discrimination, it is likely that many studies tend to underestimate numbers. However, government actuaries estimate that six per cent of the population, around 3.6 million people, are lesbian, gay or bisexual.

Stonewall's position is that if six per cent of the population are gay, then six per cent of those who are economically disadvantaged are likely to be gay. We also know from our research that gay people face a wide range of challenge and discrimination that can contribute to social exclusion.

Stonewall's survey of 1,658 lesbian, gay and bisexual people, *Serves You Right*, found that gay people expect poorer treatment from public services including social housing, criminal justice and health services.

> ***The general perception ... that the majority of the 'gay community' is mainly white, male and middle-class, with high levels of disposable income, does not accurately reflect the diverse backgrounds of gay people in Britain***

Serves You Right also found that nearly one in five gay people say they have experienced bullying from their colleagues because of their sexual orientation. Discrimination in the workplace can lead to people leaving their jobs and becoming unemployed. Lesbian, gay and bisexual people in occupational groups C2DE (working class) are 50 per cent more likely to experience bullying than those in occupational groups ABC1 (middle class).

Stonewall's survey of 1,140 young lesbian, gay and bisexual people, *The School Report*, found that 65 per cent of young people had experienced homophobic bullying. Seven in ten feel this has an impact on their work, and half have skipped school at some point because of it. More broadly, Stonewall's *The Gay British Crime Survey* found one in five lesbian, gay and bisexual people have experienced a homophobic hate crime in the last three years.

Research indicates that discrimination can impact on mental health and wellbeing. Some who take claims to employment tribunals about discrimination on the grounds of sexual orientation asserted that the bullying and harassment that they had experienced caused them

STONEWALL / BITC DIVERSITY

to develop mental health problems, including anxiety and depression.

Stonewall's report on a survey of 6,000 lesbian and bisexual women, *Prescription for Change*, found that half of young women under the age of 20 have self-harmed in the last year. Research indicates that young lesbian, gay and bisexual people are more likely to be at risk of homelessness because of bullying at school and rejection from the family home. Generally, therefore, discrimination impacts on health and wellbeing. This in turn can affect social inclusion and economic wellbeing.

Stonewall often hears from lesbian, gay and bisexual people who are experiencing difficulties accessing the correct benefits via our freephone information service. This is often because local authorities and benefits offices get confused about the rights of same-sex couples. Many organisations are still not clear on the rights and responsibilities of lesbian, gay and bisexual people, which can lead to heightened economic exclusion.

Research also clearly demonstrates that women are more likely to experience lower economic wellbeing than men as a result of lower pensions, and fewer opportunities to access education, employment and training. These circumstances are likely to be exacerbated for two women who live together, rather than a man and a woman. This aspect of economic deprivation is often overlooked by government and policy makers.

What we have done

From 2009, national government datasets have started to include a question relating to sexual orientation. Stonewall lobbied for this change and welcome it. In future, this will mean more accurate data will be available on the social exclusion faced by lesbian, gay and bisexual people.

However, as questions relating to sexual orientation are relatively new, it is anticipated that it will take several years to secure completely accurate data.

Furthermore, the Office of National Statistics found when testing the questions that people who have no educational qualifications, belong to a lower socio-economic group or come from a deprived neighbourhood are more likely to answer 'prefer not to say' in response to a question relating to sexual orientation.

What we are currently doing

Stonewall continue to work with government and respond to consultations on social exclusion and deprivation where relevant to lesbian, gay and bisexual people.

For example, we engage with the independent National Equality Panel tasked with investigating the relationships between different aspects of inequality in people's economic situations, and their other characteristics and circumstances.

There are complex interactions both between multiple equality strands and also wider conditions of economic and social disadvantage. We recognise that more in-depth research into the social exclusion and economic disadvantage experienced by lesbian, gay and bisexual people is needed and we continue to work to develop appropriate research methodologies in this challenging area.

If you require more information on Stonewall's work in social exclusion please contact 08000 50 20 20 or info@stonewall.org.uk

⇨ The above information is reprinted with kind permission from Stonewall. Visit www.stonewall.org.uk for more information.

© Stonewall

STONEWALL

Attitudes and stereotyping towards LGBT people in the EU

Extract from Homophobia, transphobia and discrimination on grounds of sexual orientation and gender identity in the EU Member States: Summary of findings, trends, challenges and promising practices.

> ***Council of Europe Recommendation CM/Rec(2010)5 of the Committee of Ministers to Member States on measures to combat discrimination on grounds of sexual orientation or gender identity***
>
> 8. Public officials and other state representatives should be encouraged to promote tolerance and respect for the human rights of lesbian, gay, bisexual and transgender persons whenever they engage in a dialogue with key representatives of the civil society, including media and sports organisations, political organisations and religious communities.

Research findings

Attitudes of the general public and the strategy of 'invisibility'

Attitudes of the general public towards lesbian, gay, bisexual and transgender (LGBT) persons across the EU vary from one member state to another. There is evidence to suggest that attitudes are influenced by age (younger people being more tolerant than old), political inclination (left wing being more tolerant than right wing), sex (women being more tolerant than men) and education (the more educated being more tolerant than the less educated). Existing national surveys suggest that attitudes towards LGBT persons vary according to the context. For instance, a general tolerance of LGBT persons as potential 'neighbours' does not necessarily translate into the acceptability of LGBT persons being able to marry or adopt children.

According to the findings of the Special Eurobarometer survey on discrimination in the EU of November 2009, almost half of EU respondents (47%) think that discrimination on grounds of sexual orientation is widespread in their country.[1] This indicates a slight improvement compared with the equivalent findings of 2008, when 51% of EU respondents perceived sexual orientation discrimination as widespread.[2] It appears relatively rare for individuals to have LGBT friends and acquaintances: the EU average stood at 38% in 2009, with the highest rate in the Netherlands (68%) and the

lowest rate in Romania (3%). Using a ten-point 'comfort scale' (with ten indicating most comfortable), individuals were asked to indicate their level of comfort with an LGBT person holding the highest political office. The EU average was 6.5 points, with Sweden (8.7), Denmark (8.4) and the Netherlands (8.2) scoring highest, and Romania (3.4) and Bulgaria (3.2) scoring lowest.

> 'Hetero-normative' describes the attitude that heterosexuality – that is, attraction towards people of a different sex only – is normal, natural and superior to homosexuality – that is, attraction towards people of the same sex only – or bisexuality – that is, attraction towards people of either sex.

To avoid negative reactions, many LGBT persons adopt a strategy of 'invisibility' with co-workers, family and friends. This in itself may lead to emotional difficulties and may be connected with the higher incidences of

EUROPEAN UNION AGENCY FOR FUNDAMENTAL RIGHTS

mental health problems experienced by LGBT persons. More generally, the negative attitudes or prejudices of the population can translate into discriminatory treatment by employers, colleagues, service providers, the media, as well as political and religious leaders. While it is possible to ensure legal protection of LGBT persons against discrimination, this in itself cannot adequately address the day-to-day problems faced in a heteronormative context.

A project realised under the EQUAL programme, which was coordinated by Swedish organisations, showed that in schools, for example, everyone is assumed to be heterosexual. The project aimed to reveal 'what lies beneath the surface' and how the assumption of heterosexual exclusivity affects interactions among staff and in the classroom.[3] Research shows that social structures and institutions still work on the basis of an underlying heterosexual norm which can generate consequences at odds with a fundamental rights approach.

'Neither cultural, traditional nor religious values, nor the rules of a "dominant culture", can be invoked to justify hate speech or any other form of discrimination, including on grounds of sexual orientation or gender identity.'

Recommendation CM/Rec(2010)5 of the Committee of Ministers to Member States on measures to combat discrimination on grounds of sexual orientation or gender identity (adopted by the Committee of Ministers on 31 March 2010)

Opinion-makers contribute to shaping attitudes

Efforts are made to address the issue of homophobic or transphobic statements in media reports. For instance, the Lithuanian Gay League produced a publication to change the way LGBT issues are presented to the public.[4] In Latvia, a study has identified patterns of homophobic speech and presented a mechanism for monitoring political speeches with regard to gays and lesbians.[5] In some Member States, there are examples of church representatives and politicians who actively lobby against the adoption of rights and protection for LGBT persons or LGBT events, such as gay prides.

Identifying challenges and promising practices

Unsettled trends across the EU may reflect or reinforce negative attitudes towards LGBT people, as well as transphobic and homophobic stereotyping. A first step in addressing this issue is to identify the challenges and possible ways to promote a culture of respect and diversity inclusive of LGBT people in Europe's societies today. Enhancing public understanding and acceptance requires dialogue and engagement between governments and civil society. The FRA therefore

organised a roundtable in Naples in October 2010, bringing together various stakeholders in the field of LGBT rights such as NGOs, equality bodies, police, policy-makers and international organisations.

Challenges

Identifying key civil actors and current obstacles

The discussions of the Naples roundtable focused on the role and influence of particular institutional elements in society and found that:

⇨ media, political and religious leaders, as well as education institutions, have a key role in determining public opinion on LGBT issues;

⇨ these institutions (media, politics, religious leaders, education institutions) can often be resilient to change;

⇨ the absence of legislation securing LGBT rights undermines the possibility of challenging the continuity of particular practices and directly challenging stereotypes;

⇨ medical professionals can act as 'gate keepers' in determining access to legal gender recognition and trans-related medical treatment.

In the discussions, participants also identified several obstacles, namely:

⇨ the lack of systematic and coordinated solutions that are based on the participation of the communities they intend to benefit and are directed to their needs;

⇨ the lack of rights awareness by members of LGBT communities, and the consequent lack of empowerment to defend those rights;

⇨ reluctance among the general public to engage in diversity programmes inclusive of LGBT people, such as opposition expressed by parents to such initiatives in schools;

⇨ lack of funding for civil society organisations and other bodies capable of promoting LGBT rights, such as equality bodies. Attitudes and stereotyping towards LGBT people.

Ways forward

A number of governments throughout the EU actively promote equal rights and opportunities regardless of sexual orientation or transgender identity or expression. Negative attitudes nevertheless remain. Prejudice against LGBT persons is often based on unfounded assumptions, for example that 'homosexuality is an illness', 'LGBT persons are responsible for the collapse of traditional values' or 'homosexuality is a vice or perversion like drug addiction or paedophilia'. If such

prejudices can be countered through education and awareness-raising campaigns, it is likely, that in the long term, discrimination faced by LGBT persons will be addressed more effectively, in particular if such campaigns are supported by public authorities, such as EU institutions, and national, regional and local governments.

The media play a crucial role in improving the public perception of LGBT people, for example by avoiding homophobic statements, stimulating informed public debate and presenting more balanced portrayals of LGBT issues.

Furthermore, it is important to engage in constructive dialogue with political and religious leaders addressing concerns about the social impact of more tolerant attitudes on LGBT issues. Dialogue should also take place with bodies responsible for promoting human rights, such as national equality bodies and national human rights institutions, as well as with LGBT organisations.

Promising practice

Promoting a culture of respect and diversity inclusive of LGBT people

In Sweden, one of the tasks of the Living History Forum, a government agency with responsibility to promote democracy, tolerance and human rights, is to assist in 'combat[ing] the institutionalisation of heterosexuality in society', thereby contributing to making visible and challenging the underlying assumptions which confine LGBT people into invisibility and exclusion.[6]

The Netherlands has also adopted a comprehensive LGBT policy document for the period 2008-2011, entitled *Simply Gay*. It constitutes a national action plan encompassing 60 different measures, including 24 projects sponsored by various government departments to improve the social acceptance and empowerment of LGBT citizens.[7]

The United Kingdom has included an ambitious programme of work to 'tackle outdated prejudices and ensure equal changes for everyone, whatever their sexual orientation or gender identity' in its *Programme for Government*.[8]

Ensuring a systematic approach based on 'leadership and ownership' was highlighted as crucial in the conclusions of a thought-provoking seminar on the exchange of promising practices organised by the European Commission in March 2010.[9] Building on that, the participants of the Naples roundtable concluded that public authorities should ensure the enforcement of human rights standards by adopting an equality agenda in a top-down approach starting from a commitment by senior officials and filtering down into clear guidelines, specific procedures and training. Active consultation with

LGBT communities, as well as building up the capacity of LGBT organisations to improve their monitoring activities, would be important elements in this process. In addition, participants at the roundtable in Naples recommended inter-service dialogue and action plans on issues such as hate-motivated violence, both of which should involve the police, local authorities, schools, university, health authorities and the LGBT community. Such action plans should also focus on long-term and sustainable measures.

Encouraging acceptance of lesbians, bisexuals and gay men in public institutions

In Sweden, various organisations, including employer associations, trade unions, LGBT organisations, a municipality, a state government and the Ombudsman against sexual orientation discrimination, all coordinated and supported two projects that were funded by the EU EQUAL programme: 'Homosexuals and bisexuals in the care system' and 'Normgiving diversity'. The latter project focused on three professions that 'have a normative function and set standards in society': the police, the Church and the defence forces. The main partners of the project were employer associations, namely the Swedish Armed Forces, the Swedish National Police Board, and the Association of Parishes and Pastorates of the Church of Sweden, together with several trade unions and NGOs. Both projects produced a training tool to help create open and inclusive workplaces. The main idea of the projects was to create a working environment where every individual is respected and has equal rights, regardless of their sexual orientation.

Notes

1   See European Commission (2009c).

2   See European Commission (2008b).

3   See Under Ytan [Beneath the Surface], available at: www.ytan.se/?p=1892.

4   See Lithuanian Gay League (2007).

5   See Mozaika – an Alliance of Lesbian, Gay, Bisexual, Transgendered Persons and their Friends in Latvia (2007).

6   See Sweden/Ministry of Integration and Gender Equality (2009).

7   See the Netherlands/Ministry of Education, Culture and Science (2007).

8   See UK/Government Equalities Offices (2010).

9   See Crowley, N. (2010).

⇨ The above information is an extract from the European Union Agency for Fundamental Rights (FRA)'s report *Homophobia, transphobia and discrimination on grounds of sexual orientation and gender identity in the EU Member States*, and is reprinted with permission. Visit http://fra.europa.eu for more information.

© FRA

EUROPEAN UNION AGENCY FOR FUNDAMENTAL RIGHTS

Government to cut aid to anti-gay countries

The Government will cut aid to poor countries which persecute gay people, international development secretary Andrew Mitchell has warned.

By Jessica Geen

Aid 'fines' may be imposed on countries such as Uganda and Ghana for hardline anti-gay laws, the *Mail on Sunday* reported.

Malawi, which sentenced a couple to 14 years' hard labour for contravening anti-gay laws, has already had its aid cut by £19 million.

A spokesman for Mr Mitchell told the newspaper that the Government now regularly reviews aid-receiving countries on their commitments to human rights.

He said: 'The Government is committed to combating violence and discrimination against lesbian, gay, bisexual and transgender people in all circumstances, in this country and abroad. We take action where we have concerns.

In Ghana, a government minister recently called for the arrest of all gay people in the country's western region. This followed president John Evans Atta Mills' pledge to curb the 'menace' of homosexuality

'We now allocate funds every three months, rather than every year, so that we can review a country's performance, for example on human rights, and take swift action when governments fall short. We only provide aid directly to governments when we are satisfied that they share our commitments to reduce poverty and respect human rights.'

Prime Minister David Cameron has defended Britain's spending on foreign aid, saying that increasing the budget from £7.5 billion last year to £11.4 billion in 2013 is a sign of 'moral strength'.

In Ghana, a government minister recently called for the arrest of all gay people in the country's western region. This followed president John Evans Atta Mills' pledge to curb the 'menace' of homosexuality.

Mr Mitchell's deputy Stephen O'Brien told the president earlier this year that Ghana would lose its £36 million a year from Britain unless he stops persecuting gay people.

Uganda, which expects to receive £70 million this year from Britain, has been considering legislation to strengthen current laws against gay people.

The harshest provisions call for the death penalty in 'aggravated' cases of homosexuality, although parliament appears to have shelved the bill.

10 October 2011

⇨ The above information is reprinted with kind permission from Pink News. Visit www.pinknews.co.uk for more information.

© Pink News

WE WILL PUNISH GAYS, LESBIANS AND-

AND..?

AID

PINK NEWS

Gay: born this way?

The debate about what makes people gay has been raging for decades. Now scientists aim to settle it for good, says Jeremy Laurance.

'Sexual orientation is not a matter of choice, it is primarily neurobiological at birth.' So said Jerome Goldstein, director of the San Francisco Clinical Research Center, addressing 3,000 neurologists from around the world at the 21st meeting of the European Neurological Society (ENS) in Lisbon last month.

In doing so he was attempting to settle a debate that has raged for decades: are gays born or made? It is a puzzle because homosexuality poses a biological conundrum. There is no obvious evolutionary advantage to same-sex relationships. So why are some people attracted to others of the same sex? Sexual attraction provides the drive to reproduction – sex is a means to an end not, in Darwinian terms, an end in itself. From an evolutionary perspective, same-sex relationships should be selected out.

'Sexual orientation is not a matter of choice, it is primarily neurobiological at birth'

Despite this, they are common in the animal kingdom. Birds do it, bees probably do it and fleas may do it, too. Among the many examples are penguins, who have been known to form lifelong same-sex bonds, dolphins and bonobos, which are fully bisexual apes. Various explanations have been advanced for the evolutionary advantage that such relationships might confer. For example, female Laysan albatrosses form same-sex pairs, which are more successful at rearing chicks than single females. Homosexuality may also help social bonding or ease conflict among males where there is a shortage of females. Gay couples will not preserve their own genes but they may help preserve those of the group to which they belong.

The existence of homosexuality in the animal kingdom has been cited to demonstrate that it is not a sin against nature. The American Psychiatric Association removed homosexuality from its list of recognised mental disorders almost 40 years ago in 1973 and the World Health Organization followed suit in 1992. The UK Royal College of Psychiatrists does not produce its own list of disorders but tends to follow the WHO.

Yet as recently as February 2010, the college felt compelled to issue a statement to 'clarify that homosexuality is not a psychiatric disorder,' adding:

'There is no sound scientific evidence that sexual orientation can be changed. Furthermore, so-called treatments of homosexuality create a setting in which prejudice and discrimination flourish.'

The move was prompted by a survey of 1,400 psychiatrists and therapists, which found more than one in six had offered to help turn gays straight, or reduce their gay or lesbian feelings. Moreover, the cases were not concentrated in the past, but spread across the decades up to the present.

Professor Michael King of the University College Medical School, who led the study published in *BMC Psychiatry*, said at the time: 'We didn't expect it to be happening at this rate and we are really rather concerned ... It is distressing and harmful and there is absolutely no evidence it works.'

One puzzle was that far fewer therapists said they would attempt to change someone's sexual orientation if asked to do so – one in 25 – than admitted having actually done so. They seemed uncomfortable with giving treatment, or admitting to it. Pressure from clients demanding help because of bullying or discrimination may have pushed the therapists into delivering it.

Professor King said: 'If the therapist is not wise enough to say that this is a part of them and there is nothing pathological about it, they may get seduced into trying to change them. Instead, the therapist should be saying that it is very unfortunate they are being bullied and that they can try to help them come to terms with their situation.'

Research in neurobiology, cited by Jerome Goldstein in Lisbon last month, has served to reinforce this view. If it can be shown that the brains of gay people are physiologically different from heterosexual people, the idea that they are 'aberrant' and may be changed is harder to sustain.

Twin studies have revealed a probable genetic link with sexual orientation and Dr Goldstone plans to examine the brains of identical twins using MRI scanners for differences.

Researchers from the Karolinska Institute, Stockholm, using MRI scanners measuring blood flow to the brain have already found differences in the size of the amygdala in the brain, which plays a key role in emotional responses. The brains of homosexual men resembled those of heterosexual women and those of homosexual women resembled those of heterosexual men.

THE INDEPENDENT

The research builds on other studies of neurological differences between gay and straight men and women. A study led by Qazi Rahman at Queen Mary, University of London, found gay men and heterosexual women share a poor sense of direction and are more likely to navigate using landmarks or by asking someone. It is heterosexual men who stick stubbornly to the map.

The right-hand side of the brain dominates spatial capabilities, so may be slightly more developed in heterosexual men and lesbians. An earlier study found gay men and heterosexual women outperformed lesbians and heterosexual men in verbal fluency.

These studies hark back to those by Simon LeVay, a gay neuroscientist at the Salk Institute in San Diego, California, who claimed to have found structural differences in the brains of homosexual and heterosexual men. Post-mortems studied by LeVay revealed that a region of the brain called the interstitial nuclei of the anterior hypothalamus is two or three times bigger in heterosexual men than it is in women. In gay men, however, this region is about the same size as in women.

This supported the notion that the brains of gay men were in some ways a bit like women. But LeVay acknowledged

that it was impossible to say whether this made people gay or whether the differences in their brains were a consequence of being gay. To make a compelling case, it would be necessary to show that the neurological differences existed early in life and that it was possible to predict future sexual orientation from them.

But he was captivated by the idea that if gays were 'born that way', it could undermine the morality of homosexual discrimination. He believed that a lifestyle based on an innate propensity rather than a conscious choice is far more difficult to condemn.

Jerome Goldstein agrees. 'We must continue to bring forward data that show the differences or similarities between the brains of homosexuals, heterosexuals, bisexuals, and transgender persons.' He added: 'The neurobiology of sexual orientation and the gay brain, matched with other hormonal, genetic, and structural studies, has far-reaching consequences beyond sexual orientation.'

'Curing' homosexuality

The idea that homosexuality can be cured has a long and dubious history. For most of the last century it was thought to be an aberration from the norm that could be 'corrected', rather than a natural state. Everyone was thought to be basically heterosexual and homosexuality was regarded as a deviation, the result of 'faulty learning' in childhood.

During the 1950s and 1960s, when belief in psychological behaviourism was at its height, aversion therapy was used to 'cure' homosexuals. Male patients were given a slide show which included pictures of sexually attractive men and women and a lever that allowed them to change the slides. If they lingered too long over the pictures of the men, and did not move on swiftly enough to the pictures of the women, they received an electric shock. A variation of this treatment involved a drug that would make them vomit.

Aversion therapy, famously employed in Anthony Burgess's novel *A Clockwork Orange* to cure Alex of his obsession with violence, was used up to the 1980s, but has since been discredited.

Other treatments included advice to masturbate to a homosexual fantasy and then switch to a heterosexual one near orgasm. Covert sensitisation required patients to counter homosexual thoughts with shameful fantasies of arrest by the police or discovery by their family.

Although not uncommon, these treatments never became mainstream in Britain. In the US, however, the idea that homosexuality can be cured retains wide support.

14 June 2011

© The Independent

So do they really zap you if you look at the wrong pictures?

Don't know... I had my eyes closed!

THE INDEPENDENT

The therapist who claims she can help gay men go straight

A psychotherapist who tried to convert a gay man to become heterosexual faces being struck off at a landmark disciplinary hearing this week.

By Robert Mendick, Chief Reporter

The case will expose the growing use of hugely controversial therapies from the United States which attempt to make homosexual men heterosexual.

The therapy has been described by the leading professional psychotherapy body as 'absurd', while the Royal College of Psychiatrists said 'so-called treatments of homosexuality' allow prejudice to flourish.

A small group of counsellors believe all men are born heterosexual but that some choose a homosexual lifestyle which can then be changed through counselling.

Lesley Pilkington, 60, a psychotherapist for 20 years, faces being stripped of her accreditation to the British Association for Counselling and Psychotherapy (BACP) after treating a patient who had told her he wanted to be 'cured' of his homosexuality.

The patient was in fact a prominent homosexual rights campaigner and journalist, who secretly recorded two sessions with Mrs Pilkington, a devout Christian, before reporting her to the BACP.

Mrs Pilkington says her method of therapy – Sexual Orientation Change Efforts (SOCE) – is legitimate and effective. The therapy is practised by a handful of psychotherapists in Britain.

Mrs Pilkington, whose 29-year-old son is homosexual, said she was motivated by a desire to help others. 'He [my son] is heterosexual. He just has a homosexual problem,' she said last week.

Mrs Pilkington has accused Patrick Strudwick, the award-winning journalist who secretly taped her, of entrapment. On the tape, Mr Strudwick asks Mrs Pilkington if she views homosexuality as 'a mental illness, an addiction or an antireligious phenomenon'. She replies: 'It is all of that.'

Mr Strudwick told *The Sunday Telegraph*: 'Entering into therapy with somebody who thinks I am sick … is the singularly most chilling experience of my life.'

He added: 'If a black person goes to a GP and says I want skin bleaching treatment, that does not put the onus on the practitioner to deliver the demands of the patient. It puts the onus on the health care practitioner to behave responsibly.'

Mr Strudwick approached Mrs Pilkington at a largely Christian conference – run by the US organisation The National Association for Research and Therapy of Homosexuality – where he said he was unhappy with his homosexual lifestyle and that he 'wanted to leave it'. He then requested 'treatment for his same-sex attraction'.

In May 2009, Mr Strudwick attended a therapy session at Mrs Pilkington's private practice, based at her home in Chorleywood, Herts, and recorded the session on a tape machine strapped to his stomach.

In the disciplinary letter sent to Mrs Pilkington, she is accused by BACP of 'praying to God to heal him [Strudwick] of his homosexuality'. She is also accused of having an 'agenda that homosexuality is wrong and that gay people can change and that you allegedly attempted to inflict these views on him'.

Mrs Pilkington told *The Sunday Telegraph*: 'He told me he was looking for a treatment for being gay. He said he was depressed and unhappy and would I give him some therapy.

'I told him I only work using a Christian Biblical framework and he said that was exactly what he wanted.'

She estimates that in the past decade she has offered the SOCE method to about one patient a year, lasting typically about a year.

'We don't use the word "cure" because it makes it [homosexuality] sound like a disease. We are helping people move out of that lifestyle because they are depressed and unhappy.

'We say everybody is heterosexual but some people have a homosexual problem. Nobody is born gay. It is environmental; it is in the upbringing.'

The SOCE method involves behavioural, psychoanalytical and religious techniques. Homosexual men are sent on weekends away with heterosexual men to 'encourage their masculinity' and 'in time to develop healthy relationships with women', said Mrs Pilkington.

'It would be absurd to attempt to alter such fundamental aspects of personal identity as sexual orientation by counselling'

She said she became involved in 'this lifestyle treatment' because of her son. 'I am not in this because I am judging people. I am in it because I understand what the issues are.

'I have been able to help my son. We have gone through a process in my family. I want to help others who are in a similar place.

'[My son] is still gay ... we are developing a relationship that was quite difficult for many years but is now coming back in a very nice way. I am confident he will come through this and he will resolve his issues and that he will change.'

Her legal defence is being funded by the Christian Legal Centre (CLC), which has instructed Paul Diamond, a leading religious rights barrister, to fight the case.

Andrea Minichiello Williams, the director of the CLC, said: 'It is shocking that Lesley was targeted, lied to and misrepresented by this homosexual activist and even worse that her professional body consider her actions worthy of investigation.

'Therapy should remain freely available for those who wish to change their homosexual behaviour.'

The Royal College of Psychiatrists issued a policy statement last year condemning conversion therapies. It stated: 'There is no sound scientific evidence that sexual orientation can be exchanged. Furthermore, so-called treatments of homosexuality create a setting in which prejudice and discrimination flourish.'

Philip Hodson, a fellow of the BACP, said: '[BACP] is dedicated to social diversity, equality and inclusivity of treatment without sexual discrimination or judgmentalism of any kind, and it would be absurd to attempt to alter such fundamental aspects of personal identity as sexual orientation by counselling.'

16 January 2011

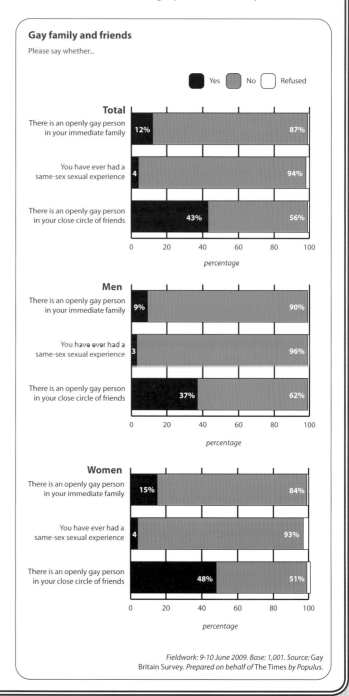

Gay family and friends

Please say whether...

Yes   No   Refused

Total

There is an openly gay person in your immediate family: 12% / 87%

You have ever had a same-sex sexual experience: 4 / 94%

There is an openly gay person in your close circle of friends: 43% / 56%

percentage

Men

There is an openly gay person in your immediate family: 9% / 90%

You have ever had a same-sex sexual experience: 3 / 96%

There is an openly gay person in your close circle of friends: 37% / 62%

percentage

Women

There is an openly gay person in your immediate family: 15% / 84%

You have ever had a same-sex sexual experience: 4 / 93%

There is an openly gay person in your close circle of friends: 48% / 51%

percentage

Fieldwork: 9-10 June 2009. Base: 1,001. Source: Gay Britain Survey. *Prepared on behalf of* The Times *by* Populus.

THE DAILY TELEGRAPH

Trans terminology

Information from Channel 4 and Flamingo.

Transgender/Trans

(adj) An umbrella term describing people who feel the need to present themselves to the world in a gender other than the one they were assigned at birth. Transgender people may go on to describe themselves as transsexual, transvestite, crossdressers, intersex or by a number of other terms (including, simply, man or woman).

Transvestite

(adj, occ n) A person who wears the clothing of the gender opposite to the one they were assigned at birth, but does not feel the requirement to live permanently in that role, and does not fundamentally question the gender with which they were assigned at birth.

Transsexual

(adj) A person who holds the belief that they should be living full time in the gender role opposite to that assigned to them at birth may be said to be transsexual (NB not 'a transsexual'). Transsexual people often (though not always) take steps to change their bodies to reflect their deeply-held understanding of their inner gender.

Gender Reassignment Surgery

Transition

(n, vi) The process of moving from living in one gender to living in the other, usually undertaken by transsexual people. Transitioning involves major social and emotional adjustment, and can be a period of great stress and vulnerability.

> ***[Transgender or trans is] an umbrella term describing people who feel the need to present themselves to the world in a gender other than the one they were assigned at birth***

Crossdresser

(n) An alternative word for 'transvestite', a crossdresser is a person who wears the clothing of the gender opposite to the one they were assigned at birth, but does not feel the requirement to live permanently in that role, and does not fundamentally question the gender with which they were assigned at birth.

Drag queen/king

(n) A person who dresses in the clothes of the gender opposite to the one in which they live for much of the time, often for performance reasons. People who use these terms as the primary way of describing themselves may be less likely to be gender dysphoric, and are often entirely content to live in their assigned gender role.

FtM

(adj) Female to Male. Describes a person who is transitioning from living as a female to doing so as a male.

MtF

(adj) Male to Female. Describes a person who is transitioning from having lived as a male to living as a woman.

CHANNEL 4 / FLAMINGO

Gender Affirmation Surgery (GAS)

(n) The best term to use to cover the range of medical interventions a transitioning person may undertake. Gender Confirmation Surgery is also used. Gender Realignment Surgery is in wide use but is less accurate. Sex Reassignment Surgery is now obsolete, and sex change is inappropriate.

Gender dysphoria

(n) An underlying and incessant disquiet or anxiety centred on the understanding that who you are is not reflected by the gender of your body.

Gender Identity Disorder (GID)

(n) Another term for gender dysphoria. Widely disliked by trans people as the word 'disorder' marginalises and pathologises rather than simply recognises difference.

Gender Identity Clinic

(n) A specialist NHS clinic to which transgender people may eventually be referred by their GP after presenting with the symptoms of gender dysphoria.

Gender Recognition Act (GRA)

(n) 2004 legislation which gives transsexual people who have transitioned full legal rights as a member of the gender in which they are living, including the right to have their birth certificate revised, and to marry.

Genderqueer

(adj) Individuals who call themselves genderqueer may regard themselves as having aspects of either gender, or none. They will typically feel uncomfortable with using language that fits into a binary definition of gender.

Gender variant

(adj) A general term that describes all those who express their gender in a way at odds with society's 'normalised' male or female, or those who feel they are not described by this binary.

Intersex

(adj) A medical term covering a range of recognised conditions, which create an ambiguity around the physical sex of an individual.

Real Life Experience/Real Life Test

(n) Clinical protocols recommend that a transsexual person transitioning must live for one year in their 'new' gender, full-time and uninterrupted, before being referred for GAS. In England, the NHS adopted a two-year system: elsewhere it is one year.

Transgender or trans umbrella

Transsexual women (Male to female) Transsexual men (Female to male) Intersex people Androgyne and polygender people Cross-dressing and transvestite people

It is currently common to use the terms 'transgender people' or 'trans people' as 'umbrella' terms to cover the many diverse ways in which people can find their personal experience of their gender differs from the assumptions and expectations of the society they live in.

As transgender people have become more widely known and written about, various terms have developed in an attempt to highlight similarities and differences. However, individuals will still always view themselves, and experience their lives, in unique ways.

Source: Scottish Transgender Alliance*

* Note: While the Scottish Transgender Alliance shows various more specific terms under the 'transgender' or 'trans' umbrella, this does NOT mean that we think ALL people who identify with one of these specific terms will also see themselves as being transgender or trans. It ONLY means that SOME people who identify with those more specific terms may see themselves as part of the umbrella.

Terms to avoid

Sex change

(n, adj) Transitioning individuals are confirming their gender, not 'changing their sex'. 'Sex change' and 'sex swap' are widely regarded as offensive.

Tranny

(n) While still a term that may be used within the trans community (with understanding, or ironic affection), use by those outside it has come to be seen as highly abusive by most trans people.

Pre-op

(n, adj) Many trans people detest having their experience reduced to a surgical event. Using 'pre-op' (as in 'pre-op transsexual') implies that 'post-op' is the more valid status. It also adds to the impression that transsexual people need to be labelled by others.

⇨ Information from Channel 4 and Flamingo. Please visit www.channel4.com and www.flamingoresearch. co.uk for more.

© Channel 4/Flamingo

CHANNEL 4 / FLAMINGO

'My trans daughter'

Information from NHS Choices.

Sharon has a teenage daughter who is transgender. She describes how Nicki was born in a male body but felt from a very young age that she should have been a girl.

'When my child Nick was about two, I realised that he wasn't playing with toys that I expected a boy to play with. He was interested in dolls and girly dressing-up clothes. At that age, it doesn't really matter. You just think they're trying lots of different things, so I never made a fuss about it.

'But when he was four years old, Nick told me that God had made a mistake, and he should have been a girl.

'I asked my GP what I should do. He told me to wait and see, and that it might just be a phase and go away. But it didn't. It got stronger.

'One day when Nick was six, we were in the car, and he asked me when he could have the operation to cut off his "willy" and give him a "fanny". His older cousin had told him about these things.

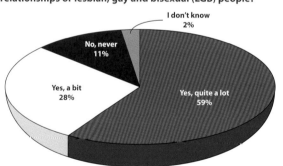

At your school, have you ever been taught about same-sex relationships or lesbian, gay and bisexual (LGB) people?

I don't know 2%
No, never 11%
Yes, a bit 28%
Yes, quite a lot 59%

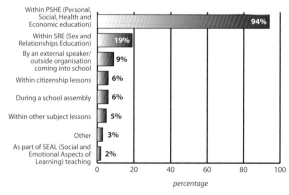

How were you taught about same-sex relationships or lesbian, gay and bisexual (LGB) people?

	percentage
Within PSHE (Personal, Social, Health and Economic education)	94%
Within SRE (Sex and Relationships Education)	19%
By an external speaker/ outside organisation coming into school	9%
Within citizenship lessons	6%
During a school assembly	6%
Within other subject lessons	5%
Other	3%
As part of SEAL (Social and Emotional Aspects of Learning) teaching	2%

Source: Tackling homophobia and transphobia in settings supporting young people: What are the barriers and facilitators? Findings from a South Yorkshire study. *Sheffield Hallam University, 2011*

'I spoke to a friend who's a psychiatrist. He said I should contact the Tavistock Clinic [now The Tavistock and Portman service for children and young people with gender identity issues].

'He also told me that the medical term is "gender dysphoria". When I looked it up online, I found Mermaids, a charity that helps children with gender identity issues and their families.

'I also spoke to my GP again, who referred us to the local mental health unit. The person at the unit had worked at the Tavistock and knew about gender identity issues.

> ## *Nicki was born in a male body but felt from a very young age that she should have been a girl*

'He was brilliant. It was such a relief to talk to somebody who understood what was going on. I'd blamed myself, but he reassured me that it wasn't my fault. We were then referred to the Tavistock Clinic.

'The team from the Tavistock came to Nick's school and talked to the teachers. They helped the teachers to understand that Nick wasn't being difficult, and that this may or may not be a phase. When a child is this young, you just don't know.'

From Nick to Nicki

'Nicki desperately wanted to be female all the time. When she was ten, we feminised her name from Nick to Nicki at home. The following year, Nicki started secondary school as a girl.

'The school was very supportive, but because she moved up to secondary school with her peer group, everybody knew.

'In the first week, she was called a "tranny" and a "man-beast". She was spat on and attacked in the corridors. Within her first six months of being at that school, she took four overdoses.

'We then pulled her out of school, but after a few months she decided to go back.

'Each year, the bullying and isolation got worse, and Nicki started harming herself. At the beginning of year nine, I transferred her to another secondary school, but unfortunately the kids there found out.

'At that point, I withdrew her from school completely, and the education welfare office found her a place at a Specialist Inclusive Learning Centre, which is a unit

for children who can't cope with mainstream schooling for various health reasons.'

Going through puberty

'When Nicki started puberty, I wanted her to get the type of treatment that's offered in the Netherlands, where puberty is blocked before major physical changes take place.

'I felt that if she was going to change her mind about being a girl, she would have done so by now.

'The Tavistock Clinic wouldn't give her hormone blockers. [The Tavistock and Portman follows British guidelines, which at the time suggested not introducing hormone blockers until the latter stages of puberty. Since January 2011, the age at which hormonal treatment may be offered has been lowered from 16 to 12, under a research study that is being carried out by the Tavistock and Portman into the effects of hormone blockers earlier in puberty.]

'In the end, we went to a doctor in the US. I found him through the WPATH network The World Professional Association for Transgender Health. Nicki was 13 when she started taking hormone blockers. It's put her male puberty on hold, and given her time to think.

'If she hadn't been given blockers, she would have suffered the psychological agony of going through male puberty. She told me she would have killed herself. Nowadays, you'd never guess that she was born male.

'If at any point Nicki told me that she wasn't sure that this was the right thing for her, we'd simply stop the injections and male puberty would go ahead.

'For Nicki, the next step is starting hormones and surgery as soon as she can.

'During the first few years of secondary school, I was constantly in fear for Nicki's life. It was so distressing to watch her go through all of this.

'Now it's a million times better. She's a typical teenage girl, and it's a blessing. She leaves a mess, she borrows my clothes, my make-up and my perfume. I never thought she'd reach this stage. She still has to face many more hurdles but she's looking forward to adulthood.'

The names in this article have been changed

Where to get help

Sharon, who tells her story above, says that the most helpful thing was speaking to other families who've been through the same thing. The charity Mermaids provides family support for children and teenagers with gender identity issues, and it can put you in touch with other parents with similar experiences.

Further information

The story above reflects one mother's experience. Because gender identity issues are complex and each case is different, Sharon's story shouldn't be seen as typical.

For more information on gender identity issues in children and young people, see the 'Teenagers and gender identity' and 'Worried about a child with gender identity issues?' pages on the NHS Choices website (www.nhs.uk).

Last reviewed 27 May 2011

⇨ Reproduced by kind permission of the Department of Health – nhs.uk

© Crown copyright 2012

NHS CHOICES

Worried about your child?

Information from NHS Choices.

If a child seems confused about their gender, it's normal for parents to feel puzzled or worried. But it's important to support your child and not to jump to conclusions.

It's common and natural for very young children to show an interest in clothes or toys associated with the opposite gender.

Children under five have little awareness that certain preferences are associated with one gender or other. If a three-year-old boy enjoys dressing in his sister's clothes, this probably means nothing in terms of how the child feels about his gender.

Even among older children, it's not uncommon for boys and girls to identify with the opposite gender or to say they want to be the opposite gender.

Mermaids, a charity that provides support and information to children with gender identity issues and their families, says that parents of younger children contact it more often about boys than about girls.

'This is probably not because gender-variant behaviour is more common in boys but because a little girl who's a tomboy tends to be less of a concern than a little boy who plays with Barbies.'

Parents tend to worry more about gender-variant behaviour in little boys because it presents more of a challenge to our assumptions about gender.

Will my child grow up to be transsexual?

Very few children who seem to be confused about their gender go on to live full-time as the opposite gender, or to be transsexual, as adults.

In most cases, the gender variant behaviour or feeling disappears as the child gets older.

Children who do continue to experience gender variance as they get older will develop in different ways. Some may feel they don't belong to any gender. Others may want to dress in the clothes of the opposite gender from time to time or on a regular basis.

Only a small number who have persistent and strong feelings of belonging to the opposite gender end up living full-time in the opposite gender.

When should I seek help for my child?

'If your child is very strongly identifying with the opposite gender, to the point where it's causing the child or the family distress, seek help,' advises Ady Davis, a psychosexual therapist with the North-East Gender Dysphoria Service.

'Signs of distress in a young person or child can include self-harm, destructive behaviour and depression.'

For young people who feel strong and persistent discomfort about their gender, puberty is often a very difficult time. The physical changes that occur at puberty can increase feelings of unhappiness about their body or their gender.

If your child is strongly identifying with the opposite gender, it's best to get help before puberty begins.

If the feelings of gender discomfort persist to the extent that your son or daughter wants to live full-time in the opposite gender, careful preparation needs to be made with the school and any clubs or groups that your child attends.

Who can help?

For medical help, first visit your GP. The next step is usually referral to a local CAMHS (Child and Adolescent Mental Health Service) team, where psychological help will be offered to your child or teenager. This may involve working with the whole family, and sometimes with the school as well.

Depending on what services are available locally and on what your Primary Care Trust is willing to fund, some young people are referred to the gender identity service at Tavistock and Portman NHS Foundation Trust in London. This is the only medical centre in the UK that specialises in helping children with gender variance.

Many parents find that talking to other people who've had similar experiences is a great help in terms of finding out more about gender variance, and receiving support.

The charity Mermaids has a telephone helpline (020 8123 4819, Mon-Sat 3-7pm), which parents can call for advice, information and support. The Mermaids website also has several real stories by young people and their parents.

In what ways can I support my child?

Sometimes, children worry that if they tell you how they feel, you won't love them any more.

Mermaids' key advice to parents is: 'Accept your child and let them know that no matter what their preferences are, no matter how they feel, you support them and love them.'

Even if you feel concerned, try to be relaxed about cross-gender behaviour in your child. It's important that children don't feel judged or rejected because of who they are.

If you feel anxious or uncomfortable, you're not alone. You may blame yourself because you think it's your fault. But gender identity is nobody's fault.

Bullying

Bullying at school is often an issue for children and teenagers who behave in ways that don't fit into traditional ideas about gender roles. At primary school, the other kids may not want to play with them because 'they don't act like boys' or 'they don't act like girls'. Secondary school can be even tougher.

The family may also be bullied and victimised.

Last reviewed 27 May 2011

⇨ Reproduced by kind permission of the Department of Health.

© Crown copyright 2012

UN rights chief lauds Australian move on identity for transgender, intersex people

The United Nations human rights chief today welcomed Australia's decision to enable its citizens who are transgender or intersex, or who do not wish to identify themselves as either male or female, to have their sex and gender identity properly reflected on their passports.

'By its action, Australia has placed itself in the vanguard of change and has scored an important victory for human rights,' High Commissioner for Human Rights Navi Pillay said in a news release.

The option of expressing a change of gender or indeterminate gender will now be open to Australians who have had appropriate clinical treatment – and not necessarily physical treatment.

'This is something that will be welcome news for many transgender and intersex people in Australia who from now on will not be required to undergo surgery or hormonal treatment in order to be able to express their gender identity,' said Ms Pillay.

'Without official recognition of their preferred gender, transgender and intersex individuals face a wide range of practical, everyday challenges – for example, when applying for a job, opening a bank account or travelling,' she noted.

'Making it simpler for people to obtain official documents that reflect their preferred gender will make life easier for thousands of people, in the process removing barriers that until now have prevented them from exercising their human rights on an equal footing with others.'

According to the High Commissioner, more states are starting to recognise the need to reflect sex and gender diversity, with countries such as Nepal, Portugal, the United Kingdom and Uruguay having taken 'pioneering' steps in recent years to make it easier for transgender and intersex persons to obtain legal recognition of a change of gender, or to indicate a gender other than male or female.

She urged all states to review their laws, policies and practices to ensure that discrimination against transgender and intersex individuals is addressed in a systematic and effective way.

16 September 2011

⇨ The above information is reprinted with kind permission from the United Nations. Visit www.un.org for more information.

© UN

Well, enjoy your trip mate...errr...miss?

DEPAR

NHS CHOICES / UNITED NATIONS

Transsexual people and the public eye

What challenges would be faced by a famous person transitioning in public?

By Juliet Jacques

There are few openly transsexual people in British public life – and virtually none who have come out when already famous. The most notable exception remains acclaimed travel writer Jan Morris, who kept her gender reassignment secret until announcing its conclusion in 1972 and then publishing her autobiography, *Conundrum*. Since then, nobody approaching Morris's level of celebrity has publicly transitioned, with almost all of Britain's known transsexual people realising their identity before stepping into the spotlight.

By contrast, the hard work of post-war activists and the courage of openly gay, lesbian or bisexual people have created a climate where, slowly, public figures can discuss their sexual preferences without press intrusion – or pressure to act as advocates – ruining their lives. Since Thatcher's Conservatives passed the deplorable Section 28 in 1988, banning the 'promotion' of homosexuality in schools, progress has been remarkable: having apologised for this legislation,

David Cameron's government now retains 13 openly gay Tory MPs, and there is now a diverse range of visible gay, lesbian or bisexual people in the arts, media and, gradually, sport.

The situation for noted people in any field who come out, or are outed, as transsexual would almost certainly be less accommodating. (I focus on 'transsexual' rather than 'transgender' people, cross-dressers or transvestites, as the 'Real Life Experience' required to access medical treatment obliges full-time living in the chosen gender, making its public expression and resultant attention unavoidable). As there have been so few test cases, I can only speculate on what may unfold, but the experiences of visible transsexual people in the USA offer some clues.

> **There are few openly transsexual people in British public life – and virtually none who have come out when already famous**

Recently, at least three Americans have publicly transitioned: Sonny and Cher's son Chaz Bono, actor Alexis Arquette and *LA Times* sports writer Mike Penner, briefly known as Christine Daniels. Chaz Bono transitioned from female to male, Arquette and Penner from male to female; their contrasting fortunes, including Penner's detransition and suicide, illustrate the challenges that a British counterpart might face.

The fundamental issues would be around privacy. The concerns for anyone whose transition is picked up by the print or broadcast media have been covered previously by David Allen Green, but for our transsexual pioneer, these would be magnified by already being in the public eye.

Interest would be most intense at the point of disclosure, which could mean facing virtually every consequent social challenge simultaneously. If preparing to come out, a transsexual person would be best served telling family, friends and colleagues before the press – if secured, their support would be vital in dealing with inevitable 'curiosity'. If not, that person might think again about going public, although doing so would eventually become essential according to the gender reassignment pathway – and once made, the announcement may find its way into the public domain anyway, even if retracted.

Recorded hate crime from regional forces in England, Wales and Northern Ireland during the calendar year 2010 (all in trans and sexual orientation categories).

Avon & Somerset
Bedfordshire
Cambridgeshire
Cheshire
City of London
Cleveland
Cumbria
Derbyshire
Devon & Cornwall
Dorset
Durham
Dyfed-Powys
Essex
Gloucestershire
Greater Manchester
Gwent
Hampshire
Hertfordshire
Humberside
Kent
Lancashire
Leicestershire
Lincolnshire
Merseyside
Metropolitan
Norfolk
North Wales
North Yorkshire
Northamptonshire
Northumbria
Nottinghamshire
PSNI
South Wales
South Yorkshire
Staffordshire
Suffolk
Surrey
Sussex
Thames Valley
Warwickshire
West Mercia
West Midlands
West Yorkshire
Wiltshire

0   300   600   900   1200   1500

number of crimes

Source: Association of Chief Police Officers (ACPO)

Total hate crimes motivated by homophobia and transphobia in 2010

5,240

THE INDEPENDENT

If outed by someone else, around the start of the process, that person would not have the reassurance that loved ones could be relied upon for backing – and may have no idea who to ask for help. (Anyone who did come out today might seek out Trans Media Watch as a first point of contact, as they provide support to people whose gender status is widely known.) Either way, the Real Life Experience would have to begin at some point – and the scrutiny of his or her appearance, if not entire life, would start.

'Before and after' pictures have long been a staple in media coverage of transsexual people, alongside undermining of the identity chosen. This is not to mention the possibility of speculation about personal and professional relationships or mental health, or intimate questions about sexuality, genitalia and surgery – something that activist Christine Burns, for example, had to manage in television appearances – all when this person would feel most vulnerable, striving on several fronts to assert his or her true self.

'Before and after' pictures have long been a staple in media coverage of transsexual people, alongside undermining of the identity chosen

For those with little connection to other similar people or any grounding in trans politics or theory, some challenges may come as an unpleasant surprise. Chaz Bono and Alexis Arquette both spent plenty of time within LGBT circles before transition and probably knew what types of attack, and what support, could reasonably be anticipated not just from 'straight' conservatives, but from certain lesbian or gay critics, and the 'transgender' community (an increasingly fractious alliance, which, like many groups struggling for social change, has sometimes been susceptible to attacking its own). One of the saddest parts of Penner/Daniels's sad story was the breakdown in relations with trans support networks over how Daniels presented as a woman, and how unprepared she was for this kind of criticism. The crucial problems, however, involved her relationships with her family – not the media.

Given the continued lack of individuals who are able – or allowed – to offer a transsexual perspective to a large audience as a counterpoint to negative coverage, a public figure might feel pressure to 'represent' people, but this role could be declined relatively easily if he or she did not feel comfortable in assuming it. Bono and Arquette both became more famous as a consequence of transition, and have often seemed more comfortable performing an advocacy function, and their patient, articulate explanations of their histories and the support they have received from family, friends and the wider public bodes well for anyone in Britain who takes similar steps. But how much has changed here since Jan Morris's day still remains to be seen.

Juliet Jacques is the author of the Orwell Prize long-listed Guardian *blog 'A Transgender Journey'.*

17 June 2011

© The Independent

Now I'm ready to come out!

THE INDEPENDENT

Equal marriage – trans perspectives

Information from Changing Attitude.

By Tina Beardsley

The announcement of a Government Consultation on Equal Marriage is to be warmly welcomed as a prelude to ending a very serious anomaly. Under present UK legislation, those trans people who were already married prior to their transition (and the implementation of the Gender Recognition Act 2004), and wish to remain so, are not allowed to obtain a full Gender Recognition Certificate, nor can they be issued with a new/amended birth certificate. In order to complete their journey, and be legally recognised as male or female, the individual concerned must obtain an Interim Gender Recognition Certificate, which has a six-month life, during which time it can be used to annul their marriage, followed by the issue of a full Gender Recognition Certificate. The couple may then, should they wish, contract a Civil Partnership, and some have done this, though many, unwilling to renege on their solemn vows, remain married but, legally at least, in gender limbo.

During the Commons reading of the Gender Recognition Bill one MP observed, 'I can think of no other circumstance in which the State tells a couple who are married and who wish to remain married that they must get a divorce', and some MPs objected to this requirement as inhumane and destructive of the family. In spite of this opposition the Bill was carried with this provision intact because of the perception, at that stage, that the country was not ready for equal marriage. To allow couples to remain married, after one had transitioned, would have created same-sex marriage by default, and to do so would have undermined the case for Civil Partnerships – the legislation for which was being debated at the same time – namely, that Civil Partnerships were not the same as heterosexual marriage.

This Government, it seems, is prepared to review that, and quite rightly, as experience, seven years on, does suggest that many people in this country have come to regard civil partnerships as marriage in all but name, and the notion of a difference – apart from the gender of the persons – unconvincing. The commitment and love, the sacrifices and compromises are all more or less the same. Prior to the Civil Partnership Act, faithful same-sex couples existed in significant numbers, but the legislative change has made their relationships more public and far better known.

'Hetero-normative' is the concept that comes to mind to describe the thinking that led to the cruel dilemma that requires a married trans person to divorce in order to become fully who they are. It resembles the old protocol that used to insist that a trans person first divorce in order to access treatment; the assumption being that their sexuality would realign with their gender after transition: the mistaken belief that both prior to and after treatment they would be attracted to people of the 'opposite' sex. But that outcome cannot be assumed.

Ironically, it was those trans people who were in a same-sex relationship prior to transition (and whose sexual orientation has remained constant) who have benefited most from the current legislation, and who were the first to be married, whether in church or the registry office – their joy tinged with sorrow at the impossible choice being faced by their married friends.

These are matters I addressed at 'Come Out & Play 2011', the LGBT Human Rights Summit and the LGBT Health Summit in Cardiff earlier this month, where I joined lawyer Erich Hou, Su Rathgeben Knan of Liberal Judaism, Tony Green and Sharon Ferguson of LGCM and Peter Tatchell of Outrage on the Equal Marriage Panel to consider the legal and religious overview. At the press conference that preceded it I commented that Changing Attitude's current campaign is 'Civil Partnerships in Church Now!' and that Changing Attitude fully supports the Equal Marriage Campaign.

18 September 2011

⇨ The above information is reprinted with kind permission from Changing Attitude. Please visit http://changingattitude.org.uk for more information.

© Changing Attitude

CHANGING ATTITUDE

Discrimination on grounds of sexual orientation

Information from the Coventry Law Centre.

Since 1 December 2003 it has been unlawful to discriminate against somebody at work on the grounds of their sexual orientation. The new law applies to all employment and vocational training and includes recruitment, terms and conditions, promotions, transfers, dismissals and training at work. Sexual orientation is broadly defined as orientation towards persons of the same sex (gay men and lesbians), orientation towards persons of the opposite sex (heterosexual) or orientation towards a person of the same sex and the opposite sex (bisexual).

What type of discrimination is covered?

Direct discrimination

Direct discrimination occurs when a worker or a job applicant is treated less favourably on grounds of their sexual orientation or perceived sexual orientation. So, if somebody Is not employed, or is dismissed, or is not provided with training or promotion, or given unfavourable terms and conditions of employment, or denied access to other benefits, purely on the grounds of their sexual orientation then this will amount to direct discrimination.

In some limited circumstances there may be a Genuine Occupational Requirement (GOR) that a job is undertaken by a person of a particular sexual orientation. For example, a charity providing advice exclusively to lesbians and gay men may consider it more credible to have a lesbian or a gay man as the manager of the organisation. Alternatively, some religious organisations may refuse to employ somebody on the grounds of their sexual orientation on the basis that it is incompatible with their religious belief. However, GORs are always open to challenge by an individual and the burden of proof lies with the employer to establish the validity of a GOR by providing evidence to substantiate the claim. Employers should be very careful when suggesting there is a GOR.

Indirect discrimination

Indirect discrimination occurs when a company or organisation applies a provision, criterion or practice which applies to all workers and job applicants regardless of sexual orientation but puts persons of the same sexual orientation at a particular disadvantage when compared with other persons, and which cannot be shown to be a proportionate means of achieving a legitimate aim.

For example, a policy requiring workers and job applicants to disclose all criminal convictions (including spent criminal convictions) could be discriminatory in light of the fact that certain consensual homosexual acts were once illegal.

Indirect discrimination will not be unlawful if it can be justified. An employer must be able to show that there is a legitimate aim, in other words a real business need, and that the practice is proportionate to that aim. In other words, there is no alternative to the provision, criterion or practice which is in place.

Harassment

Harassment consists of any behaviour that undermines the dignity of the individual and is offensive, frightening or in any way distressing. This can include intentional bullying, which would be obvious, but it can also be more subtle, such as nicknames, teasing or name-calling. Such behaviour can cause great upset to the individual and the employer is under an obligation to investigate and treat seriously allegations of harassment.

Victimisation

Victimisation occurs when an individual received detrimental treatment because they have made a complaint, they intend to make a complaint or it is a third party who is assisting somebody who has made a complaint to a tribunal.

Liability

An employer should be liable for the actions of its employees, or other third parties if they are in a position to control the situation or take remedial action. If they do not do so then you may have a valid claim against them.

Enforcement of the law

The way that the law against discrimination on grounds of sexual orientation is enforced is by complaint to an

COVENTRY LAW CENTRE

employment tribunal. However, before a complaint is made to a tribunal it is advisable to make sure that you have exhausted all internal grievance procedures. A complaint to a tribunal must be made within three months of the act complained of or if the complaint is of a succession of acts, within three months of the last act committed.

It is worth seeking legal advice at an early stage to determine whether you have a case in law and the strength of your case.

⇨ Information from the Coventry Law Centre. Visit www.covlaw.org.uk for more information.

Homophobic crime

If you are a victim of crime and think that you were targeted because of your sexuality, or the sexuality of someone you know, find out about how the police will help you when you report it.

What is homophobic crime?

If someone becomes a victim of crime because of their sexuality, then this is classed as a crime where homophobia is one of the main motivations.

Homophobic hate crime can happen anywhere and is often based on prejudice and stereotypes. Any homophobic crime will be taken very seriously by the police. Sentences for crimes proven to have a homophobic motive behind them will be tougher and the reporting of homophobic crimes will be treated as seriously as racial hate crimes.

Types of homophobic crime

Homophobic crime can affect victims in many ways. For example, someone could be assaulted or robbed because their attacker does not like people who they see as different to them.

Other victims may have homophobic graffiti and slogans painted on their house or belongings by people who suspect that someone who lives there is gay.

Reporting a homophobic crime

If you have been a victim of a crime, or witnessed a crime taking place, and you think that there may have been a homophobic motive behind it, you should mention this to the police when you are giving your statement.

Victims of homophobic crime may be reluctant to report the incident to the police because they are not comfortable talking about their sexuality to people they do not know. They may feel that they will not be listened to or taken seriously.

Most local police forces have a special unit that is dedicated to dealing with incidents of homophobic crime. Officers who work in these units have had special training on how to deal with issues of homophobia. If you would feel more comfortable talking to someone like this, ask to speak to them when you contact the police station.

Homophobic bullying

If you are still at school, you may be bullied because others think you are gay. Although this is not a crime that you can report to the police, being bullied is still an upsetting experience and you shouldn't put up with it.

Bullying doesn't just happen at school. You may be being harassed, victimised or picked on at work because your colleagues think you're gay.

Whether you are at school or work, you should let a teacher or a manager know if you're being bullied so that they can do something about it.

⇨ The above information is reprinted with kind permission from Directgov. Visit www.direct.gov.uk for more information.

Homophobia exacts a chilling price as hate crimes climb

People having sex changes are the new targets.

By Emily Dugan and James Bloodworth

Hate crime towards gay and transgender people is on the rise across Britain, with thousands of people suffering abuse for their sexuality every year. Crimes against transgender people went up by 14 per cent during 2010 and, in some cities, attacks motivated by sexual prejudice are up by as much as 170 per cent annually.

The rise in homophobic crime in England, Wales and Northern Ireland went from 4,805 offences in 2009 to 4,883 in 2010. Campaigners say the figures are just the 'tip of the iceberg' as research suggests three out of four people are still too afraid to report these crimes.

The police now record any crimes they believe are motivated by homophobia – anything from persistent harassment to serious assault and murder. Experts believe the reason for the increase may be in part because more people feel able to be open about their sexuality, making them easier to be picked out by thugs. Vic Codling, national co-ordinator of the Gay Police Association, said: 'People have got more confidence in themselves and, when you get people who are openly gay, that provokes homophobes. There is still stigma in Britain and, if you're open about your sexuality, that encourages people to take up arms and act on homophobia.'

The gay rights group Stonewall says there is anecdotal evidence that unprovoked attacks on lesbian, gay, bisexual and transgender (LGBT) people are on the rise. The results can be fatal. The story of 62-year-old Ian Baynham, who was killed by drunken teenagers screaming 'Faggot' while they bludgeoned him to death in London's Trafalgar Square in September 2009, is one of many. *The Independent on Sunday* is aware of at least nine people who have been killed by attackers because of their sexuality – or who committed suicide after being bullied – since 2009.

A growth in more extremist religious views has also contributed to the increase in attacks. A homophobic campaign, launched by extremist Muslims in east London earlier this year, featured stickers declaring the area a 'gay-free zone' and that Allah would be 'severe in punishment'. 'A lot of the problems come when people believe their religion encourages them to be homophobic,' said Mr Codling.

The rise in recorded attacks may partly be attributable to an increasing willingness among the LGBT community to go to the police and report crime. Police have also been better trained in recording crimes as homophobic, rather than just robberies or muggings.

The most dramatic increase is in Scotland, where homophobic abuse has risen fivefold in five years, police statistics show. There were 666 crimes against LGBT people recorded in Scotland in 2009/10 – almost double the 365 reported in 2007/08.

In Oxford, homophobic crimes reported to police rose by more than 170 per cent last year; and in London's West End, still a focal point for the capital's gay nightlife, crimes motivated by homophobia increased by 20.9 per cent.

Experts say a dramatic growth in the number of transgender people seeking medical sex changes has made those born into a different gender more visible and therefore more vulnerable. In 2010, there were 357 incidents of hate crime against transgender people, up 14 per cent from 2009. The number of people medically changing their sex is growing at a rate of around 15 per cent every year: 1,200 people now undergo gender realignment procedures annually.

There he goes... well-spoken, well-mannered, and well-dressed. He must be gay!

Yeah... nothing like your average bloke around here!

Bernard Reed, of the Gender Identity Research and Education Society, said: 'The more people who feel the need to reveal their condition, the more people put themselves at risk. Our research shows 90 per cent of transgender people do not report abuse, so this is the tip of a very large iceberg. Society's acceptance and understanding of trans people is up to 20 years behind LGB; we know people who are spat at every day.'

Crimes against transgender people went up by 14 per cent during 2010 and, in some cities, attacks motivated by sexual prejudice are up by as much as 170 per cent annually

While numbers of reported incidents rise, police forces nationwide are closing down specialist LGBT liaison officer posts in response to budget cuts.

Sam Dick, of the charity Stonewall, believes the problem starts in school. 'I think there's a misconception that because the laws have changed, social attitudes towards gay people have changed. But it's clear that people are leaving school feeling that homophobia and violent homophobia is acceptable: 17 per cent of gay students who have experienced homophobic bullying have received death threats. It's clear this behaviour is going on in schools unchallenged.'

Lynne Featherstone, the Equalities minister, said: 'Targeting a person purely because of gender identity or sexual orientation is a shameful act and will not be tolerated. We are working with the police to improve our response to hate crime. For the first time, forces are recording data centrally, which will help target resources more effectively and better protect victims. Everyone should have the freedom to live without fear of hostility or harassment.'

Case studies

Rachel Maton, 56: Egham, Surrey

Rachel has suffered systematic abuse since she began her sex change in 2007.

'I became a target because I'm transgender. Youths would pelt my house with eggs, smash my windows and shout at me. One day, I was hit from behind and the lights went out. Then they set upon me. My nose was smashed flat and I couldn't breathe. Now I'm careful not to get in a vulnerable position.'

Chas Anderson, 20: East London

Chas, a former model, was assaulted in April outside a gay bar in Clapham.

'My partner and I were queuing at a cash point after leaving the bar when a group started making abusive comments. They started saying the shorts I was wearing looked ridiculous, and one of them said that because I was gay, I deserved to be dead. Next thing, a man punched me in the face and I fell to the ground. There was a lot of blood and I had to go to hospital. The police said there had been a spike in similar incidents at the time in Clapham and south London.'

23 October 2011

© The Independent

Clarke: hate crime laws extended

People who murder disabled or transgender people in hate crime attacks will face life sentences with a starting point of 30 years, Justice Secretary Kenneth Clarke said today.

The Ministry of Justice plans to amend the Criminal Justice Act 2003 so that murders motivated by hatred or hostility towards disabled or transgender people will have the same starting point as for murders aggravated by race, religion and sexual orientation. This will double the current starting point for disability and transgender hate crime murders.

The Act will also be updated so that where any offence is shown to be motivated by hostility towards the victim on the grounds of transgender, as well as race, religion, sexual orientation and disability, sentences must be made more severe.

Mr Clarke said:

'Hate crimes are abhorrent, they leave sections of society living in fear and at risk of unprovoked violence. The courts already treat all hate crime seriously and aggravate sentences accordingly.

'These proposals make clear offenders should be in no doubt that they face a more severe sentence for these unacceptable crimes.'

8 December 2011

⇨ Information from the Ministry of Justice. Visit www.justice.gov.uk for more.

© Crown copyright

THE INDEPENDENT / MINISTRY OF JUSTICE

New push for LGB and T equality

Today the Government announced, as part of its commitment to advancing equality for lesbian, gay, bisexual and transgender (LGB&T) people, that religious buildings will be allowed to host civil partnership registrations.

The change, which will be entirely voluntary and will not force any religious group to host civil partnership registrations if they do not wish to do so, is being introduced as part of the Equality Act. It will give same-sex couples who are currently prevented from registering their civil partnership in a religious setting the chance to do so.

As the Home Secretary says: 'This Government is committed to both advancing equality for LGB&T people and ensuring religious freedom for people of all faiths – which is why we will be allowing religious organisations to host civil partnership registrations if they choose to do so'.

The Government's LGB&T action plan, which was published last year, included a commitment to look at next steps for civil partnerships, and giving religious organisations the right to host registration is the first stage in that process.

We have also identified a real desire to move forwards to equal civil marriage and partnerships, and will be consulting further as to how legislation can develop, working with all those who have an interest in the area.

Over recent months I have spoken to many LGB&T people and campaign groups, and it quickly became clear that there is a real desire to address the differences between civil marriage and civil partnerships.

I have always been completely clear that equal rights means exactly that – the same rights, not different rights

So I am very, very pleased to be able to announce that we are going to be the first British Government to formally look at what steps can be taken to address this.

17 February 2011

⇨ The above information is reprinted with kind permission from Lynne Featherstone MP. Please visit www.lynnefeatherstone.org for more information.

© *Lynne Featherstone*

Is homophobia a major issue?

Statistics on abuse and hate crime.

⇨ One in five lesbian and gay people have experienced a homophobic hate crime or incident in the last three years.

⇨ 68% of those targeted did not report the incident to anyone.

⇨ Young people aged 18 to 24 are more likely to be the target of homophobic abuse.

⇨ One in six victims of homophobic hate incidents experienced a physical assault and almost one in six experienced a threat of violence. 88% of victims experienced insults and harassment.

⇨ Three in five victims experienced a hate incident committed by a stranger under the age of 25. Nearly one in six victims were targeted by offenders who live in the local area, and one in ten were the victim of an incident committed by a work colleague.

(Source: YouGov survey commissioned by the Home Office, 2008)

Homophobic bullying is clearly recognised to be an issue by the Department for Children, Schools and Families, OFSTED, the health and police services and schools and youth groups nationwide.

⇨ Information from Educational Action Challenging Homophobia (EACH). Visit http://eachaction.org.uk for more.

© *EACH*

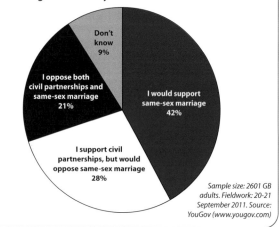

Since 2005 same-sex couples have been able to enter into civil partnerships. While civil partnerships offer the same legal rights as marriage, same-sex couples are not able to marry. Which of the following best reflects your view?

Don't know 9%

I oppose both civil partnerships and same-sex marriage 21%

I would support same-sex marriage 42%

I support civil partnerships, but would oppose same-sex marriage 28%

Sample size: 2601 GB adults. Fieldwork: 20-21 September 2011. Source: YouGov (www.yougov.com)

Equal Love case goes to European Court

Legal bid for gay marriages and heterosexual civil partnerships.

'Eight British couples will formally file a joint legal application to the European Court of Human Rights this Wednesday, 2 February, in a bid to overturn the twin bans on gay civil marriages and heterosexual civil partnerships,' announced human rights campaigner Peter Tatchell of the LGBT human rights group OutRage!.

The European Court challenge will be formally announced at a meeting in Committee Room 17 at the House of Commons at 10.30am, booked in the name of Caroline Lucas MP. Ms Lucas is the keynote speaker.

Prior to this meeting, there will be a photo call at 9.30am, where the couples filing the European Court challenge will post their application in the red letterbox at the corner of Abingdon Street and Great College Street, SW1, diagonally opposite the House of Lords.

Peter Tatchell is coordinator of the Equal Love campaign – www.equallove.org.uk – which seeks to end sexual orientation discrimination in both civil marriage and civil partnership law.

'Since November, four same-sex couples were refused marriage licenses at register offices in Greenwich, Northampton and Petersfield. Four heterosexual couples were also turned away when they applied for civil partnerships in Islington, Camden, Bristol and Aldershot,' added Mr Tatchell.

'All eight couples received letters of refusal from their register offices, which we are now using as the evidential basis to challenge in the European Court of Human Rights the UK's exclusion of gay couples from civil marriage and the prohibition of straight civil partnerships. Since there is no substantive difference in the rights and responsibilities involved in gay marriages and heterosexual civil partnerships, there is no justification for having two mutually exclusive and discriminatory systems.

'Outlawing black or Jewish people from getting married would provoke uproar. The prohibition on gay marriages should provoke similar outrage. Arbitrarily excluding heterosexual couples from civil partnerships is equally reprehensible.

'The bans on same-sex civil marriages and opposite-sex civil partnerships are a form of sexual apartheid – one law for gay couples and another law for heterosexual partners. Two wrongs don't make a right. In a democratic society, we should all be equal before the law,' said Mr Tatchell.

Wednesday's launch will be chaired by Peter Tatchell, and feature Caroline Lucas MP as the keynote speaker, plus some of the eight couples and their legal advisor, Professor Robert Wintemute of the School of Law at Kings College London. He will outline the legal basis of the Equal Love challenge to the current proscriptions.

'Our Equal Love campaign wants both marriages and civil partnerships opened up to all couples, different-sex and same-sex. Let everyone have a free and equal choice,' said Professor Wintemute.

'Banning same-sex marriage and different-sex civil partnerships violates Articles 8, 12 and 14 of the European Convention on Human Rights.

'It's discriminatory and obnoxious, like having separate drinking fountains or beaches for different racial groups, even though the water is the same. The only function of the twin bans is to mark lesbian and gay people as socially and legally inferior to heterosexual people.

'I am confident that we have a good chance of persuading the European Court of Human Rights that the UK's system of segregating couples into two "separate but equal" legal institutions violates the European Convention. I predict that same-sex couples will be granted access to marriage in the UK and that this will be because the UK Government will eventually accept that it cannot defend the current discriminatory system,' he said.

Countries, provinces and states with marriage for same-sex and different-sex couples:

17 – Argentina, Belgium, Canada, Iceland, Netherlands, Norway, Portugal, South Africa, Spain, Sweden, USA (Connecticut, Iowa, Massachusetts, New Hampshire, Vermont, District of Columbia), Mexico (Federal District).

Countries, provinces and states with civil partnership for same-sex and different-sex couples:

11 – Australia (Australian Capital Territory, New South Wales, Tasmania, Victoria), Canada (Québec), Netherlands, New Zealand, South Africa, USA (Illinois, Nevada, District of Columbia).

Countries, provinces and states with both marriages and civil partnerships open to gay and heterosexual couples, i.e. 'Equal Love':

3 – Canada (Québec), Netherlands, South Africa.

31 January 2011

⇨ Information from the Equal Love campaign. Visit http://equallove.org.uk for more.

EQUAL LOVE

Foster parents defeated by the new Inquisition

Eunice and Owen Johns are a God-fearing Christian couple, married almost 40 years, who offered a secure and loving family home to foster children aged between five and ten. But they are to be denied the opportunity to do so any longer because they are unwilling to promote a homosexual lifestyle to a child. Neither Mr nor Mrs Johns has anything against gay people but they are not in favour of sex before marriage, whatever an individual's orientation. Their views were denounced by Ben Summerskill, of the homosexual pressure group Stonewall, as 'old-fashioned'. Yet not that long ago they would have been considered mainstream and they are, in any case, the strongly-held religious views of the couple.

The reason that they were even asked about their views on homosexuality was because Parliament passed the Sexual Orientation Regulations, making it an offence to discriminate on the grounds that someone is heterosexual, homosexual or bisexual. These are the same laws under which Peter and Hazelmary Bull, Christian owners of a guest house, were fined last month for refusing to let a gay couple share a room. But in the case of Mr and Mrs Johns, where is the victim? They were not turning anyone away. Quite the contrary – they were offering a home to children who will otherwise end up in care, and there are precious few people who will. Furthermore, since the children would be aged under ten, matters of sexuality are hardly relevant – or is it being suggested that they should be? Astonishingly, the High Court suggested that it was not so much their Christian faith as the moral certainties of the Johns that were potentially harmful to children.

There is another troubling aspect of this case. Equality laws are supposed to uphold the rights to religious belief. Yet the High Court ruled that laws protecting people from discrimination because of their sexual orientation 'should take precedence' over the right not to be discriminated against on religious grounds. Why has it been left to judges to decide whose rights trump those of others? This should have been decided by Parliament but, yet again, another sloppily-drafted measure will have far-reaching consequences for freedom of conscience in this country. Already the Roman Catholic Church has had to close its adoption agencies because they cannot conform to the law. Perhaps there is a historical irony here, because we are witnessing a modern, secular Inquisition – a determined effort to force everyone to accept a new set of orthodoxies or face damnation as social heretics if they refuse. Parliament and the courts should protect people like Mr and Mrs Johns, but have thrown them to the wolves. It is a disgrace.

28 February 2011

Gay adoption in the UK

A poll commissioned by Barnardo's and released on 31 January 2011 shows that one in three people do not think gay couples can parent as well as heterosexual couples.

However, Barnardo's strongly feels that there is no room for discrimination when it comes to potential adopters and foster carers.

Can gay people adopt?

Barnardo's wants to hear from anybody who wants to find out more about fostering or adoption. We do not exclude anyone from consideration on the grounds of sexual orientation, race, marital status, gender, disability or employment status.

Our views on gay adoption

Barnardo's chief executive Anne Marie Carrie says:

'The poll not only highlights a disturbing and prevalent belief system, but also a deepening concern that children in the care system are continuing to lose out on potential parents.

'Society's attitude plays a pivotal role in discouraging people from considering adoption. The idea that gay parents are second best must be challenged. To suggest that a same-sex couple is not as able to raise a child as a heterosexual couple is at once absurd and unsubstantiated. To continue to discourage potential adopters simply because of their sexual orientation is severely diminishing the chances of securing loving, stable homes for the children who are waiting.

'This debate needs to be urgently raised and myths surrounding how sexuality, race, marital status and gender can affect your parenting dispelled.'

31 January 2011

⇨ Information from Barnardo's. Visit www.barnardos.org.uk for more.

Gay couple's hotel battle is latest case of religion clashing with human rights

Stephen Preddy and Martyn Hall's legal victory against a Christian hotel that refused them a double room is part of a growing trend of cases that pit faith against discrimination.

By Afua Hirsch, Legal Affairs Correspondent

If there is one clear trend in contentious litigation in recent months, it is the increase in cases that pit the rights of religious communities against the prohibition on discrimination.

'Religitigation', as it is becoming known, is manifest in increasingly diverse ways. Last year Christian registrar Lillian Ladele failed to exempt herself from the duty of conducting civil partnerships, Christian counsellor Gary McFarlane lost his attempt to be exempt from giving same-sex couples relationship therapy and Christian British Airways employee Nadia Eweida lost her claim to have the right to wear a crucifix at work.

It is not only Christians in the dock. Also last year, north London's Jewish Free School lost its supreme court bid to refuse admission to a pupil on the basis of his mother's background after the court found the policy amounted to race discrimination.

In much the same vein, Christian hoteliers Peter and Hazel Bull last week lost their claim to be entitled to refuse double-bed hotel rooms to civil partners Martyn Hall and Steven Preddy. Judge Andrew Rutherford, sitting at Bristol county court, found it was 'clear that homosexuals as a group are disadvantaged by the practice adopted by [Peter and Hazel Bull].'

The case appears to be the first to try the distinct legal question of whether a civil partnership is the legal equivalent of marriage, as far as discrimination is concerned. The Bulls' case was that they openly discriminated on marital status – unmarried heterosexual couples were also denied rooms with double beds – but that this policy was based on sex outside wedlock, not sexual orientation. As their counsel memorably stated, the policy 'has nothing to do with sexual orientation but everything to do with sex'.

That argument might have been successful if it were legally accurate to compare an unmarried couple with same-sex civil partners. But anticipating arguments such as these, the law faces the issue head on. The regulations that ban discrimination against sexual orientation state explicitly that 'the fact that one of the persons is a civil partner while the other is married shall not be treated as a material difference'.

This exact issue is the subject of a separate legal campaign. Campaigner Peter Tatchell has announced that eight couples will apply to the European Court of Human Rights to overturn the law, on the basis that it 'creates a system that segregates couples into two separate legal institutions, with different names but identical rights and responsibilities ... based on their sexual orientations'.

His gripe is that same-sex couples are denied the right to marry, while heterosexuals are denied the right to civil partnerships – and that both are violations of their rights.

So while some are fighting for gay marriage, the Bulls' case confirms that, in the meantime, Christians will have to accept that civil partnerships are intended to be its equivalent as far as the law is concerned. But the interesting issue in this case lurks in the judge's commentary. 'It is no longer the case that our laws must, or should, automatically reflect the Judaeo-Christian position,' said Rutherford: that is, in regarding marriage as the only form of legally recognised binding relationship.

It is this issue that concerns religious groups – the ability of the law to move on from its religious roots to a more equitable formula of guaranteeing fundamental rights, including the right against discrimination. Of course where those rights come into conflict, a more nuanced exercise of balancing takes place – one that the judiciary has so far approached with the utmost seriousness. Rutherford confessed he found the Bulls' case 'very difficult', and Lord Phillips – President of the Supreme Court and the UK's most senior judge – said earlier this year that the Jewish school decision had been the hardest of his judicial life.

That has been of little consolation to religitigants, however. What they seem to want is a trump card that puts them above the subtle considerations of fairness. And that, the courts have repeatedly said, is not going to happen.

⇨ This article first appeared in *The Observer*, 23 January 2011.

THE OBSERVER

Sexual health and gay charities welcome lift on lifetime gay blood ban

The Government has announced that the rule regarding the eligibility of gay and bisexual men to donate blood has changed.

There will no longer be a lifetime ban, but a one-year deferral if sexually active – that means gay or bisexual men who have had oral or anal sex with a man in the last 12 months still cannot give blood.

The changes will apply in England, Scotland and Wales. The ban remains in Northern Ireland where research is still being carried out.

The National LGB&T Partnership (The Lesbian & Gay Foundation, LGBT Consortium, ELOP, London Friend, GMFA, TREC, PACE, Derbyshire Friend, Yorkshire Mesmac, GADD, GIRES and Stonewall Housing) comment:

'The Partnership is committed to reducing health inequalities, and challenging homophobia and transphobia within public services, so we welcome today's landmark decision to end the lifetime gay blood ban.

'However, the new policy still means that gay or bisexual men who have had oral or anal sex with a man in the last 12 months cannot donate blood.

'The report by the Advisory Committee on the Safety of Blood, Tissues and Organs (SaBTO), which has prompted these changes, found that the introduction of a 12-month deferral would maintain the safety of the blood supply, and bring the criteria for men who have sex with men in line with those for other groups that are at an increased risk of carrying blood-borne infections.

'Gay and bisexual men, as a group, are at higher risk of acquiring some blood-borne infections (such as HIV or Hepatitis B) than the majority of the UK. The priority of the National Blood Service is to prevent blood containing HIV or other blood-borne viruses from being passed on.

'Gay and bisexual men are determined to change the situation by working to reduce the level of blood-borne virus within the gay community.

'New figures released by the Health Protection Agency this month have highlighted that gay and bisexual men are at the greatest risk, with the largest ever number of new recorded cases of HIV in 2010.

'The Partnership is committed to raising awareness of safer sex and HIV testing within the lesbian, gay, bisexual and transgender (LGB&T) community. Condoms and lube still provide the best possible defence against HIV

and sexually transmitted infections (STIs), and it is vital that all gay and bisexual men know their HIV status and attend regular sexual health checks – many which offer a vaccination for Hepatitis B.

'More investment is needed in prevention work to ensure current services can continue to promote sexual health within LGB&T communities.

'Increased awareness around sexual health will lead to earlier diagnoses of HIV and other STIs and a reduction in HIV transmissions.

'Gay and bisexual men can donate blood stem cells and bone marrow: however, people with HIV cannot. Also, there are no restrictions preventing HIV negative gay men from donating organs.

'Today's changes are a step in the right direction, but as a community we must work together for a reduction in HIV and Hepatitis B cases, to ensure when the next review comes around we are no longer an at-risk group and see full equality.'

Carl Burnell, Chief Executive of GMFA, the gay men's health charity, comments:

'The removal of the ban to a one-year deferral is great news but it's going to leave some gay men frustrated that they still can't donate blood. However, the one-year deferral is based on scientific evidence to ensure the safety of the blood supply in relation to Hepatitis B and HIV. Gay men can play their part in ensuring the UK has a safe supply of blood for everyone, including gay men, by adhering to the one-year deferral.

'It will be news to most that Hepatitis B, rather than HIV, has kept the deferral period to one year. Hepatitis B is completely preventable if you get vaccinated against it, and I'd urge all gay men to do so. If all gay men get vaccinated against Hepatitis B, and prevalence of Hepatitis B falls in our community as a result, it would be appropriate to re-examine the evidence and reduce the deferral period even further!'

Deborah Jack, Chief Executive of NAT (National AIDS Trust), comments:

'The lifetime ban on gay men donating blood has been at the centre of much controversy and debate in recent years, particularly as it became clear that this rule and current science were completely out of sync.

'NAT was instrumental in securing a proactive, time-based review of the present lifetime bans on blood donation and we are delighted to see the review's recommendations for change being implemented.

'This decision is now based on evidence and the safety of the blood supply will be maintained. However, we are adamant that this decision will need to be reviewed again in the future as science and the HIV epidemic evolves, and new evidence emerges. We must ensure that changes in these areas are proactively monitored so that we avoid having out-dated rules in place that do not benefit the public and instead simply discriminate against certain groups.'

Sir Nick Partridge, Chief Executive of the Terrence Higgins Trust (THT), comments:

'We welcome this decision, which is based on strong new evidence that all the experts are agreed on. These regulations will ensure the safety of the blood supply for all of us while also being fair and equal in their application. We can now detect blood-borne viruses earlier and have more understanding of them, and the change reflects that.

'The remaining deferral regulation for sexually active gay men is based on their heightened risk, as a group, of sexually acquired blood-borne viruses. Changing that depends on reducing gay men's risk of HIV and other STIs to the same level as the rest of the population, and re-emphasising the vital importance of safer sex as far too many gay men still become infected with HIV

each year. We will continue to campaign to improve gay men's sexual health to a level where the regulations can be the same for all, regardless of sexuality.'

Ben Summerskill, Stonewall Chief Executive, comments:

'We recognise this move as a step in the right direction and we welcome undertakings from the National Blood Service that they will in future treat gay people with greater courtesy than they've often done in the past. We also welcome the fact that those HIV charities which doggedly supported the ban until recently have revised their position.

'However, Stonewall will continue to push for a donation system based on the real risks a potential donor poses. People wanting to donate blood should be asked similar questions – irrespective of their sexual orientation – that accurately assess their level of risk of infection. Sadly, the proposed new system will still fail to do this.'

8 September 2011

⇨ The above information is reprinted with kind permission from the National LGB&T Partnership. Visit www.lgf.org.uk for more information.

© *National LGB&T Partnership*

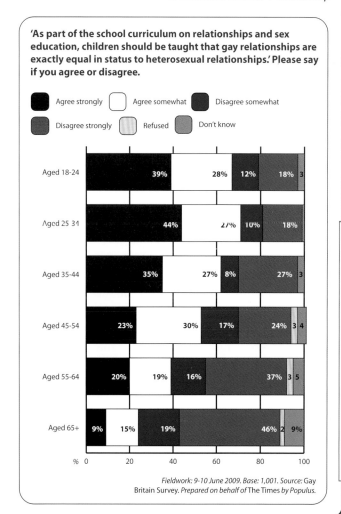

'As part of the school curriculum on relationships and sex education, children should be taught that gay relationships are exactly equal in status to heterosexual relationships.' Please say if you agree or disagree.

■ Agree strongly □ Agree somewhat ■ Disagree somewhat
■ Disagree strongly ▨ Refused ▨ Don't know

Age	Agree strongly	Agree somewhat	Disagree somewhat	Disagree strongly	Refused	Don't know
Aged 18-24	39%	28%	12%	18%	3	
Aged 25-34	44%	27%	10%	18%		
Aged 35-44	35%	27%	8%	27%	3	
Aged 45-54	23%	30%	17%	24%	3	4
Aged 55-64	20%	19%	16%	37%	3	5
Aged 65+	9%	15%	19%	46%	2	9%

% 0   20   40   60   80   100

Fieldwork: 9-10 June 2009. Base: 1,001. Source: Gay Britain Survey. *Prepared on behalf of* The Times *by Populus.*

NATIONAL LGB&T PARTNERSHIP

First kiss seals end to 'don't ask, don't tell'

Two female US sailors have become the first same-sex couple to share the traditional dockside 'first kiss' since the US ended a ban on gays in the army.

Two women sailors became the first to share the coveted 'first kiss' on the pier after one of them returned from 80 days at sea, in a navy tradition caught up with the repeal of the US military's 'don't ask, don't tell' rule.

Petty Officer 2nd Class Marissa Gaeta of Placerville, California, descended from the USS Oak Hill amphibious landing ship and shared a quick kiss in the rain with her partner, Petty Officer 3rd Class Citlalic Snell of Los Angeles.

Gaeta, 23, wore her dress uniform while Snell, 22, wore a black leather jacket, scarf and blue jeans. The crowd screamed and waved flags around them.

'It's something new, that's for sure,' Gaeta told reporters after the kiss.

'It's nice to be able to be myself. It's been a long time coming.'

[The women] met as roommates at training school and have been dating for two years, which they said was difficult under 'don't ask, don't tell'

Navy officials said it was the first time on record that a same-sex couple was chosen to kiss first upon a ship's return.

Sailors and their loved ones bought $US1 raffle tickets for the opportunity. Gaeta said she bought $US50 of tickets, a figure that she said pales in comparison to amounts that some other sailors and their loved ones had bought.

There was little to differentiate this kiss from countless others when a Navy ship pulls into its home port following a deployment. Neither the Navy nor the couple tried to draw special attention to what was happening and many onlookers waiting for their loved ones to come off the ship were busy talking among themselves.

Snell smiled as she approached Gaeta and they briefly embraced as a small contingent of local television crews and photographers, who were unaware about what was going to happen until moments earlier, captured the scene.

'She told me about the first kiss a couple of days ago and I kind of freaked out - in a good way - but of course I'm a little nervous, you know. But I've been waiting since she left,' Snell said.

David Bauer, the commanding officer of the USS Oak Hill, said that Gaeta and Snell's kiss would largely be a non-event and the crew's reaction upon learning who was selected to have the first kiss was positive.

'It's going to happen and the crew's going to enjoy it. We're going to move on and it won't overshadow the great things that this crew has accomplished over the past three months,' Bauer said.

The ship returned to Joint Expeditionary Base Little Creek-Fort Story following an 80-day deployment to Central America.

The crew of more than 300 participated in exercises involving the militaries of Honduras, Guatemala Colombia and Panama as part of Amphibious-Southern Partnership Station 2012.

Both women are Navy fire controlmen, who maintain and operate weapons systems on ships. They met as roommates at training school and have been dating for two years, which they said was difficult under 'don't ask, don't tell'.

Repeal of the 18-year-old legal provision, under which gays could serve as long as they didn't openly

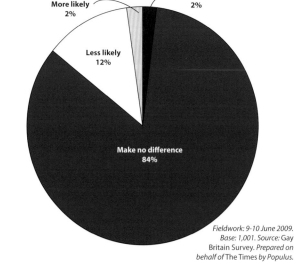

Would you be more likely or less likely to vote for a political party that you generally sympathised with, if the party leader was openly gay – or would it make no difference at all to your likelihood of voting for them?

More likely 2%
Don't know 2%
Less likely 12%
Make no difference 84%

Fieldwork: 9-10 June 2009. Base: 1,001. Source: Gay Britain Survey. Prepared on behalf of The Times by Populus.

SYDNEY MORNING HERALD

acknowledge their sexual orientation, took effect in September.

'We did have to hide it a lot in the beginning,' Snell said.

'A lot of people were not always supportive of it in the beginning, but we can finally be honest about who we are in our relationship, so I'm happy.'

The raffle money was used to host a Christmas party for the children of sailors and Gaeta said everybody in her chain of command and on her ship supported her win in the drawing.

Snell said she believes their experience won't be the last one for gays and lesbians in the military.

'I think that it's something that is going to open a lot of doors, for not just our relationship, but all the other gay and lesbian relationships that are in the military now,' she said.

Snell is based on the USS Bainbridge, the guided missile destroyer that helped rescue cargo captain Richard Phillips from Somali pirates in 2009.

22 December 2011

⇨ The above information is reprinted with kind permission from the Sydney Morning Herald. Visit www. smh.com.au for more information.

© *Sydney Morning Herald*

Factbox: lesbian, gay, bisexual and transgender rights around the world

May 17 is International Day against homo- and transphobia. Here is a snapshot of the state of legal rights of lesbian, gay, bisexual and transgender people globally.

By Astrid Zweynert

⇨ Homosexuality is illegal in 76 countries, including five that have the death penalty (Mauritania, Sudan as well as 12 northern states in Nigeria and the southern parts of Somalia, Iran, Saudi Arabia, Yemen).

⇨ Incitement to hatred based on sexual orientation is prohibited in just 24 countries.

⇨ Africa has gone from bad to worse in the past ten years, with 36 countries now having laws criminalising homosexuality. They are: Algeria, Angola, Botswana, Burundi, Cameroon (1972), Comoros, Egypt, Eritrea, Ethiopia, Gambia, Ghana, Guinea, Kenya, Lesotho, Liberia, Libya, Malawi, Mauritania, Mauritius, Morocco, Mozambique, Namibia, Nigeria, São Tomé and Principe, Senegal, Seychelles, Sierra Leone, Somalia, Sudan, Swaziland, Tanzania, Togo, Tunisia, Uganda, Zambia, Zimbabwe.

⇨ More than half of Asian and Middle Eastern countries still criminalise homosexuality but there have been some notable steps in India, where gay sex was decriminalised in 2009, and Nepal and Pakistan recognising the third gender. Homosexuality is illegal in Afghanistan, Bangladesh, Bhutan, Brunei, some parts of Indonesia (South Sumatra and Aceh Province), Iran, Kuwait, Lebanon, Malaysia, Maldives, Myanmar, Oman, Pakistan, Qatar, Saudi Arabia, Singapore, Sri Lanka, Syria, Turkish Republic of Northern Cyprus (internationally unrecognised), Turkmenistan, United Arab Emirates, Uzbekistan, Yemen, as well as the Palestinian Territories.

⇨ In Latin America and the Caribbean homosexuality is illegal in Antigua and Barbuda, Barbados, Belize, Dominica, Grenada, Guyana, Jamaica, St Kitts and Nevis, St Lucia, St Vincent and the Grenadines, Trinidad and Tobago.

⇨ None of the European countries can claim to provide full legal equality for lesbian, gay, bisexual and transgender people but Cyprus, Italy, Latvia, Malta, Turkey and Ukraine are the countries ranking the lowest in terms of legal equality.

Source: The International Lesbian, Gay, Bisexual, Trans and Intersex Association, 2011

⇨ Information from TrustLaw: www.trust.org

© *TrustLaw*

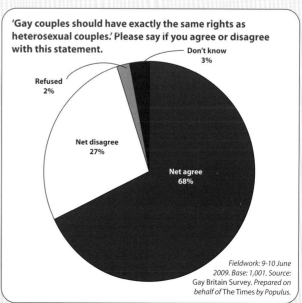

'Gay couples should have exactly the same rights as heterosexual couples.' Please say if you agree or disagree with this statement.

- Don't know 3%
- Refused 2%
- Net disagree 27%
- Net agree 68%

Fieldwork: 9-10 June 2009. Base: 1,001. Source: Gay Britain Survey. Prepared on behalf of The Times by Populus.

SYDNEY MORNING HERALD / TRUSTLAW

⇨ Many people become aware of gay feelings during their teenage years, as this is when they begin to learn more about their sexuality and identity. (page 1)

⇨ The term 'transgender', which is often abbreviated to 'trans', is an umbrella term for people whose gender identity and/or gender expression differs from their birth sex. (page 5)

⇨ In 2004 it was estimated that there were 124,672 same gender-attracted pupils in British secondary schools. (page 5)

⇨ Figures vary over how many adults identify as lesbian, gay or bisexual but an estimate that is often used is the figure of one in ten. (page 6)

⇨ Lesbians, gay men and bisexuals comprise around 6% of the population or 3.5 million people according to government estimates. (page 9)

⇨ 74% of gay and 42% of straight consumers are less likely to buy products from companies that hold negative views of lesbians and gay men. (page 9)

⇨ Stonewall's report of a survey of 6,000 lesbian and bisexual women, *Prescription for Change*, found that half of young women under the age of 20 have self-harmed in the last year. (page 10)

⇨ According to the findings of the Special Eurobarometer survey on discrimination in the EU of November 2009, almost half of EU respondents (47%) think that discrimination on grounds of sexual orientation is widespread in their country. (page 11)

⇨ In Ghana, a government minister recently called for the arrest of all gay people in the country's western region. This followed president John Evans Atta Mills' pledge to curb the 'menace' of homosexuality. (page 14)

⇨ Very few children who seem to be confused about their gender go on to live full-time as the opposite gender, or to be transsexual, as adults. In most cases, the gender variant behaviour or feeling disappears as the child gets older. (page 23)

⇨ The option of expressing a change of gender or indeterminate gender will now be open to Australians who have had appropriate clinical treatment – and not necessarily physical treatment. (page 24)

⇨ David Cameron's Government now retains 13 openly gay Tory MPs. (page 25)

⇨ Since 1 December 2003 it has been unlawful to discriminate against somebody at work on the grounds of their sexual orientation. The new law applies to all employment and vocational training and includes recruitment, terms and conditions, promotions, transfers, dismissals and training at work. (page 28)

⇨ If someone becomes a victim of crime because of their sexuality, then this is classed as a crime where homophobia is one of the main motivations. (page 29)

⇨ The rise in homophobic crime in England, Wales and Northern Ireland went from 4,805 offences in 2009 to 4,883 in 2010. Campaigners say the figures are just the 'tip of the iceberg' as research suggests three out of four people are still too afraid to report these crimes. (page 30)

⇨ People who murder disabled or transgender people in hate crime attacks will face life sentences with a starting point of 30 years, Justice Secretary Kenneth Clarke has said. (page 31)

⇨ One in five lesbian and gay people have experienced a homophobic hate crime or incident in the last three years. 68% of those targeted did not report the incident to anyone. (page 32)

⇨ A poll commissioned by Barnardo's and released on 31 January 2011 shows that one in three people do not think gay couples can parent as well as heterosexual couples. (page 34)

Bisexual

Someone who identifies as bisexual or 'bi' is attracted, romantically, emotionally and sexually, to people of either sex. While a bisexual person may be equally attracted to men and women, this does not have to be the case: they may feel a stronger attraction to one sex than the other, or feel attraction to different sexes at different points in their lives.

Civil partnership

The Civil Partnership Act 2004 (CPA) allowed same-sex couples the right to form legal partnerships for the first time, giving them rights comparable to those of married couples. A civil partnership is a legal relationship exclusively for same-sex couples, distinct from marriage. There are now calls, notably from the Equal Love campaign, to extend civil marriage and civil partnership to both same- and opposite-sex couples. The Government has launched a consultation on this issue.

Coming out

'Coming out' or 'coming out of the closet' happens when an LGBT person feels ready to tell their friends and family about their sexual orientation. As heterosexuality is the most common sexual orientation, those close to them will probably have assumed they were straight. Coming out is a big step for many gay people, especially if they fear a negative reaction from some people. It is quite common for gay people to not be fully 'out', and only let certain people know about their sexuality.

Heterosexual

Someone who identifies as heterosexual is attracted exclusively to people of the opposite sex to themselves. Heterosexuality is the most common sexual orientation. It is often referred to as 'straight'.

Homophobia

Homophobia is the fear or hatred of homosexuality and homosexual people. Individuals who are homophobic fear or hate the fact that others are sexually attracted to members of their own sex. This fear can lead to behaviour that discriminates against LGB people and consequently advantages heterosexuals. Such discrimination is illegal under the Equality Act 2010.

Homosexual

Someone who identifies as homosexual is attracted exclusively to people of the same sex as themselves. People of this sexual orientation may prefer to call themselves gay, or a lesbian if they are female. While some gay people may use other words such as 'queer' or 'dyke' to describe themselves, these are not considered universally acceptable and other gay people may find them offensive, especially if used by non-LGBT people.

LGBT

LGBT stands for Lesbian, Gay, Bisexual and Transgender, and is often used as a shorthand way of referring to sexual orientations or gender identities other than heterosexual. Just LGB (Lesbian, Gay and Bisexual) may also be used.

Pink

The colour pink is often prefixed to terms describing issues concerning gay people. A reference to the 'pink pound', for example, will concern marketing to gay people and how this group is likely to spend its money. The 'pink vote' concerns which political parties gay people are likely to support in elections.

Sexual orientation

Sexual orientation refers to an enduring pattern of emotional, romantic and/or sexual attractions to men, women or both sexes. Sexual orientation also refers to a person's sense of identity based on those attractions, related behaviours and membership in a community of others who share those attractions.

Transgender or 'trans'

A transgender or trans person is someone who identifies as the opposite gender to the one they were assigned at birth, and who has chosen to live their life in what they feel is their correct or real gender. They may or may not choose to go through gender affirmation surgery at any point. Someone's gender identity is separate from their sexual orientation: however, issues concerning transgender people and their rights tend to be discussed alongside issues affecting LGB people, as trans people often suffer similar kinds of discrimination and prejudice to LGB people.

ACKNOWLEDGEMENTS

The publisher is grateful for permission to reproduce the following material.

While every care has been taken to trace and acknowledge copyright, the publisher tenders its apology for any accidental infringement or where copyright has proved untraceable. The publisher would be pleased to come to a suitable arrangement in any such case with the rightful owner.

Chapter One: Sexual Orientation

Am I gay? Are you born gay? Can you stop being gay?, © AVERT, *Parents' stories,* © FFLAG, *Being LGB or T at school,* © Centre for Studies on Inclusive Education, *Social exclusion and sexual orientation,* © Stonewall, *The business case for diversity,* © BITC Diversity, *Attitudes and stereotyping towards LGBT people in the EU,* © European Union Agency for Fundamental Rights (FRA), *Government to cut aid to anti-gay countries,* © Pink News, *Gay: born this way?,* © The Independent, *The therapist who claims she can help gay men go straight,* © Telegraph Media Group Limited 2011.

Chapter Two: Trans Issues

Trans terminology, © Channel 4/Flamingo, *'My trans daughter',* © Crown copyright is reproduced with the permission of Her Majesty's Stationery Office, *Worried about your child?,* © Crown copyright is reproduced with the permission of Her Majesty's Stationery Office, *UN rights chief lauds Australian move on identity for transgender, intersex people,* © UN, *Transsexual people and the public eye,* © The Independent, *Equal marriage – trans perspectives,* © Changing Attitude.

Chapter Three: LGBT People and the Law

Discrimination on grounds of sexual orientation, © Coventry Law Centre, *Homophobic crime,* © Crown copyright is reproduced with the permission of Her Majesty's Stationery Office, *Homophobia exacts a chilling price as hate crimes climb,* © The Independent, *Clarke: hate crime laws extended,* © Crown copyright is reproduced with the permission of Her Majesty's Stationery Office, *New push for LGB and T equality,* © Lynne Featherstone, *Is homophobia a major issue,* © EACH, *Equal Love case goes to European Court,* © Equal Love, *Foster parents defeated by the new Inquisition,* © Telegraph Media Group Limited 2011, *Gay adoption in the UK,* © Barnardo's, *Gay couple's hotel battle is latest case of religion clashing with human rights,* © Guardian News & Media Ltd 2011, *Sexual health and gay charities welcome lift on lifetime gay blood ban,* © National LGB&T Partnership, *First kiss seals end to 'don't ask, don't tell',* © Sydney Morning Herald, *Factbox: lesbian, gay, bisexual and transgender rights around the world,* © TrustLaw.

Illustrations

Pages 8, 16, 24, 30: Don Hatcher; pages 10, 19, 26, 29: Angelo Madrid; pages 11, 17: Bev Aisbett; pages 14, 22, 27, 36: Simon Kneebone.

Cover photography

Left: © Stefano Bolognini. Centre: © Kate Northern. Right: © Marinka van Holten.

Additional acknowledgements

With thanks to the Independence team: Mary Chapman, Sandra Dennis and Jan Sunderland.

Lisa Firth
Cambridge
April, 2012

ASSIGNMENTS

The following tasks aim to help you think through the debates surrounding lesbian, gay, bisexual and transgender issues and provide a better understanding of the topic.

1 Read *Parents' stories* on pages 3-4. Coming out to parents can be a challenging time for gay and lesbian young people. In pairs, role play a scenario in which a young person tells their parents about their sexual orientation for the first time. Imagine the feelings of both parties during your conversation.

2 'This house believes that the "separate but equal" status of civil marriage and civil partnership is unacceptable in a modern, tolerant society, and that civil marriage should be legally extended to all couples.' Debate this motion in two groups, with one arguing in favour and the other against.

3 Imagine you are a therapist with a new patient who comes to you asking for help to 'cure' her of her homosexuality. How would you endeavour to help your patient understand that there is nothing wrong with her sexual orientation, and put her on her guard against therapists claiming to offer 'cures'? Role play this scenario with a partner.

4 FFLAG is an organisation which offers support and advice to the families and friends of gay people. Take a look at their website at www.fflag.org.uk. Use the information on the website and in this book to create an illustrated booklet which would help parents struggling to come to terms with their child's orientation.

5 Watch the film 'Brokeback Mountain'. Write a review, focusing on the character of Ennis and his struggle to accept his feelings for Jack in a time and society when homosexuality was not accepted.

6 Find out about the piece of legislation known as Section 28 and the reasons it was controversial. Write an account of what led to the introduction of this legislation, the arguments for and against it and what led to its repeal.

7 Read *'My trans daughter'* on pages 21-22. Write an account of these events from Nicki's viewpoint.

8 'I've got nothing against gay people personally, but I don't think it's appropriate for same-sex couples to adopt small children who may be influenced by their lifestyle choices.' Do you agree with this opinion? Hold a debate in pairs, with one person taking a supporting view and the other an opposing one.

9 In a recent campaign against homophobic bullying in schools, the charity Stonewall adopted the slogan 'Some people are gay. Get over it'. This was used on t-shirts, posters and other campaign materials. Create your own slogan to help tackle homophobic bullying and incorporate it into a poster which could be displayed in schools.

10 The number of children who are born to, or fostered/adopted by, same-sex couples is growing. However, most children's books and stories feature traditional opposite-sex family structures. Create an illustrated children's book for pre-school children which includes a same-sex parent family as part of the story (the story does not need to be about this issue, however: the aim is to make children aware that some children live within same-sex family models).

11 'When I talk to some people about being gay, they always focus on the sexual side of things. They don't seem to understand that gay relationships are just as much about emotional and romantic elements as straight ones are.' Do you think there is any truth in this statement?

12 What stereotypes exist surrounding gay men, lesbian women and transgender people? Can you think of any films or television programmes you watch, or books you have read, which perpetrate these stereotypes? Can you think of any which challenge them?

13 Think of a recent storyline in your favourite TV drama or soap which focused on the experiences of an LGBT character. Do you think the storyline was done well? Create a storyboard for your own plotline, covering an LGBT-relevant issue such as coming out, first relationships or unrequited crushes.

14 Read the novel 'Annie on my Mind' by Nancy Garden and write a review.